The Globetrotter's Guide

From Camping to Cocktails . . . The Essential Journey Planner

Amanda Statham

BOOKS

To Mum and Dad, thanks for all the help!

First published in Great Britain in 2009 by
JR Books, 10 Greenland Street,
London NW1 0ND
www.jrbooks.com

A catalogue record for this book is available from the British Library.

ISBN 978-1-906217-97-6

1 3 5 7 9 10 8 6 4 2

Printed by MPG Books, Bodmin, Cornwall

CONTENTS

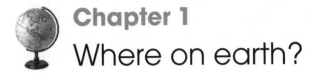

Chapter 1
Where on earth?

Travel has never been easier or more exciting. The world seems to have shrunk compared to 20 years ago, as it's now relatively easy to access and explore countries that were once seen as off-limits or only for true adventurers.

To say it's a golden age of travel may be a little optimistic, when the spotlight is shining so brightly on carbon footprints, terrorism and natural disasters, but we're certainly all travelling more than we ever have before. From short breaks in the UK to year-long work sabbaticals, it seems the Brits have got itchy feet and can't wait to jet off.

Gone are the days when the only holiday taken was a two-week summer break and time off at Christmas. These days, the average young Brit is taking up to five small breaks a year, plus increasing numbers opting for gap years, unpaid leave, work breaks and charity work overseas.

If you fall into this camp, then you've come to the right place. Whether you're plotting an adventure overseas, want some ideas and advice for a trip or simply enjoy daydreaming about spending time away, this is the book for you. Dedicated to offering as many hints and tips as possible for travellers, its aim is to be your indispensable guide through the highs and (occasional) lows of travel.

If this is your first port of call before organising a trip, then it's time to start working out the answers to four key questions: why you want to go; who, if anyone, you want to travel with; budget and, most importantly, where you want to go.

When you sit down to plan your dream trip away, whether it's for a week in the sun or a year-long jaunt, it can be daunting. The globe is, well, big, with around 195 countries to choose from (this figure includes two independent countries not in the United Nations – Kosovo and Vatican City!), which is both exciting and perplexing. Just where do you start and how do you decide which of the 195 are going to bring you the delights you crave, rather than a scary or even, dare I say it, dull travel experience.

As someone who is frequently travelling and wants to jet off again the moment I touch down, I think you could take trips your whole life and never fulfil your travel dreams. It can certainly become addictive. However, sadly it isn't possible to travel constantly, unless you've a bank account the size of Roman Abromavich's, so you need to be picky. I've devised a travel personality quiz for you (and me) to help whittle down some trip ideas – it's only a bit of fun, but it might get you thinking about the right sort of trip, and destination, for you.

QUIZ: What kind of traveller are you?

1

You never dream of travelling without your:

A – First-aid kit

B – Sense of adventure

C – Flip-flops and sun cream

D – Passport and visas

2

While you're away you'll keep in touch with home by:

A – Blogging

B – I probably won't, it'll be too remote

C – The odd phone call and text

D – Skype, it's free

3

You are best described as...

A – Capable

B – Adventurous

C – Laid back

D – Sociable

4

What do you most like to do in your spare time?

A – Read books

B – Go to the gym or something active

C – Chill out

D – See my friends

5

When you make a decision do you follow...

A – Your heart

B – Your instinct

C – Your eyes

D – Your mind

6

What sort of books do you like to read?

A – Biographies

B – Detective novels

C – Romance

D – Travel guides

7

What's your ideal holiday accommodation?

A – Simple thatched-roof hut
B – Treehouse in a jungle
C – Chic beach pad
D – A smart hostel

8

When you eat out do you prefer...

A – A restaurant serving spicy ethnic food, like Indian or Mexican
B – Somewhere new I haven't been before
C – A seafood restaurant I know and love
D – Simple, cheap food, with friends

9

What sort of transport appeals to you?

A – Foot
B – Kayak
C – Limo
D – Tuk tuk

10

How do you usually choose your holiday?

A – Reading about a destination in papers/magazines/online
B – I don't holiday, I explore
C – Recommendations from friends and family
D – Somewhere with lots to do

11

For you, when does a holiday begin?

A – Meeting the locals
B – Leaving the crowds behind
C – Feeling sand between my toes
D – Getting on the plane

12

What do you ultimately want to get out of your trip?

A - To experience a new culture, not just as a tourist

B - Excitement and a sense of achievement

C - A suntan and relaxation

D - Make loads of new friends and see lots of places

RESULTS

Mostly As

Your ideal trip = Volunteering

You're kind and caring and are really interested in the places that you travel to. You'd also like to make a difference while you're there and want to get below the tourist radar to discover what a country is really like away from hotels and resorts. You're adventurous, but not in a way that involves bungee jumping off bridges or diving with great white sharks. You're willing to try new things, from local cuisine to religious ceremonies, and won't be afraid to get stuck in and help out in local communities. Your ideal holiday would be volunteer work, such as in an African country like Botswana, Malawi, Zambia or Kenya, where you can assist with projects like constructing wells, helping in schools or monitoring wildlife. There are hundreds of volunteer schemes around the world, from India to France. See Chapter 5 for more advice on volunteer holidays.

Mostly Bs = Action and adventure travel

You don't like the idea of doing what everyone else is doing and crave an adventure that's packed full of activities and excitement. You love to travel, particularly to far-flung corners of the world, where not many tourists go. And you can keep your head about things that would leave other travellers weeping, like losing your passport. You're pretty fearless too, so there's lots of scope for adrenalin-rush antics wherever you go, whether it's white water rafting or zip-trekking (whizzing along a thin metal wire on a harness). A tour around South America is going to have you smiling, particularly really remote parts of jungle or desert. Also consider China, a vast country that is as yet very much unexplored by tourists.

Mostly Cs = Sun and sand holiday

You're a sun-worshipper and travel to you means a beach, turquoise water and near-constant sunshine. You don't particularly want to trek the Inca Trail or climb to Everest base camp, but you do want some bars, nice restaurants and fun things to do in the sun, like snorkelling. Being a sun and sand type of traveller doesn't mean you can't be adventurous – some of the most exotic places on earth also boast some of the best beaches. Australia's Gold Coast and Fiji are ideal destinations for you, and there are lots more to discover if you get the urge to be a bit of a culture vulture while you're there. The healthy, laidback outdoor lifestyle will suit you perfectly and there's the Great Barrier Reef to investigate, which is dotted with white sand-ringed islands and the most incredible marine life in the world.

Mostly Ds = Backpacking/flashpacking

You want a sociable, exciting and interesting trip and fancy travelling to several places rather than one destination. You're curious about different cultures, but want to go where you know there are going to be other likeminded souls rather than spots that are too remote. You want to be independent and not to have to rely on a fixed itinerary; if you see a place you like you want to be able to jump off the bus and stay. Making friends on your travels is important to you, as is taking care of the environment. You're made for backpacking and should head to Asia, pick up the backpacker trail and meet loads of likeminded souls along the way. From full moon parties in Koh Phangan to an Ashram in India, you'll have a ball. See Chapters 6 and 7 for more ideas.

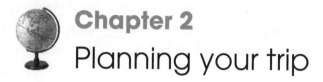

Chapter 2
Planning your trip

The anticipation of a trip can be almost as exciting as being on it. Planning all of the amazing things that you're going to be seeing and doing is part of the whole wonderful build up to your adventure. It's also essential if you're going to ensure that you make the most of your time and of the country or countries that you visit.

While it is of course fine simply to book a flight and head off into the unknown (in fact some travellers say this is the most fun way to journey), this approach isn't for the faint-hearted. Nor is it a good idea for those who don't have much travel experience, like to be in control of situations or like to do their research.

By its very nature, travel is full of the unexpected so it's wise early on to resign yourself to the fact that you're going to be subjected to surprises and experiences that weren't planned or on your itinerary – in fact these circumstances can often end up being the highlight of your hols. However, it's possible to retain elements of surprise but also to plan so that you avoid unnecessary pitfalls, such as running out of money or not having insurance if you have an accident.

BUDGET

There's no better place to start the planning process than with your budget. Whether you want to go away for two weeks or a year, you're going to need cash. If you don't have any to spare, it's not a good idea to go into debt to fund your travels. (Although it may be fun while you're away, when you've arrived home and back down to earth you don't want to be facing a mountain of debt to pay off.)

If you're short of money for your trip, start saving now. Give yourself a realistic time to put enough money aside to ensure you will be able to travel without having headaches about funding. If you're not already a dedicated saver, you'll be amazed at how quickly putting aside £100 or even £50 a month mounts up, and before you know it you'll have a nest egg to put towards your adventures. It's a good idea to set up a separate high-interest bank account to put your travel funds into – if it's combined with your general current account it's too tempting to spend the money on unrelated things, like that new pair of shoes you've got your eye on.

Set yourself a target, such as £2,000, as once you have a figure in mind it becomes really rewarding to stash a little money away each week or month and see your total climb towards the end number. You'll find that once you start saving it's quite addictive and you may start putting more aside that you originally intended.

If you're a student and not working, it's of course a different situation and harder to pull together a decent sum without having to beg and borrow. However, there are options. The first, if you aren't already doing so, is to get a part-time job in the evenings. While time as a student is as much about the social side as it is studying for some people, it's perfectly possible to get bar or restaurant work to bring in some extra funds. When I was at university I knew people who took on all kinds of extra jobs, from cleaning through to being a postman, to fund their dream trips. It's also possible to work while you're away (see Chapter 8), so don't despair if you're more in the red than the black.

In order to work out how much you're going to need to fund your travels, it's best to break your trip down into categories and work out a rough sum for each section.

Flights	£750
Transfers	£100
Accommodation	£450
Food	£225
Insurance	£35
Equipment	£50
Luggage	£50
Pre-trip vaccinations	£50
General spending	£300
TOTAL	**£2,000**

Obviously this won't be spot on, but by doing research into each category you can come up with an approximate sum, which will really help you to emerge with a final figure to aim for.

There are some fantastic flight deals on the Internet so it's well worth using comparison websites (see Chapter 17) to compare and contrast prices and make sure you get the best deals. If you're using a tour operator they will of course be able to sort out flights and transfers for you, plus accommodation too.

THE INTERNET

The Internet has revolutionised the way we travel. It's now possible to research destinations and book hotels, flights and experiences from the comfort of your armchair, but the seemingly endless choice of information on the web can make planning a trip seem very complicated.

It's pretty much a given that if you're beginning from scratch, you'll use the Google search engine (www.google.co.uk) as your starting point. However, typing in one word, such as Uganda, will produce millions of websites, most of which will be of no use to you at all. It's best to type in as many keywords as possible, such as volunteer, Uganda, summer, budget, children, to really whittle down your research area.

There are some great websites established simply to help the would-be traveller, which are worth checking out at the start of a planning session. www.tripit.com is a fantastic starting point and really good for the type of traveller who doesn't want to leave anything to chance. All you have to do is email the site your preferences, such as countries you want to travel to and when, and they'll quickly get back to you with flights, cars, trains, hotels and much more. Best of all, your itinerary automatically comes back with weather, maps and restaurant recommendations. The Big Travel Guide, www.thebigtravel guide.com, is another really useful site, offering information worldwide on everything from flights to dive companies.

Top Travel Tip

I also like www.kayak.co.uk, which allows you to plan multi-flight, multi-city trips, with hotel and transport, and it's not a travel agent so it isn't biased.

Government and tourism authority websites are also a great place to start research into a destination. They're the first place that I look when I'm investigating a potential new country to feature, as they're packed with all your vital need-to-know info. One of the downsides to the vast amount of information available on the world wide web is that not all of it is correct, much of it is out-of-date and some misleading.

The beauty of tourism authority sites are that, although written with a natural bias towards the given country ('paradise on earth' is a common phrase!), they're spot on with practical information, like when the rainy seasons is, if you need a visa and whether there's malaria. They're also very useful for providing a quick at-a-glance guide to accommodation, usually with contact information, plus a succinct round-up of the highlights of a destination.

Government websites tend to be written in a much drier style than those of the flowery tourism authority sites, but you are guaranteed the most up-to-date information and it can be more hard-hitting. I'd recommend starting with the British Foreign & Commonwealth Office (FCO)'s website, www.fco.gov.uk/travel, which will give you the low down on everywhere in the world from a Brit's perspective.

The vital information is broken down into lots of useful categories including general travel advice, how safe it is to go to countries, details of UK embassies abroad, visa require-ments, jobs overseas, health and money advice, terrorism and even what you'd need for a wedding abroad! It also offers assistance on how the FCO can help you if things go wrong when you're away, such as if you're a victim of crime, sick/injured, or arrested or detained abroad.

Basically, this site might not be glamorous (there aren't any pictures of parties on beaches or hip hotels) but it's pretty indispensable and incredibly useful for all types of travellers, from those going away for a short time to backpackers on a year-long adventure. If you do nothing else, take down details of the website address and emergency phone numbers and take these with you. For more useful websites, turn to Chapter 17.

FLIGHTS

In one way, flights have never been easier to sort out. Thanks to the Internet, it's possible to book them swiftly and simply and compare prices too. If you're willing to fly at odd times and indirectly, the savings can be massive, so it's well worth shopping around on flight comparison websites like www.opodo.com or, my favourite, www.skyscanner.net.

However, if you're searching for multiple flights it can become more of a headache. For a start the costs really start to mount up.

If you're a student or under 26, STA Travel (www.statravel. co.uk) guarantees to beat any airfare you've been offered. Their fares for flights are generally as low as you'll get anywhere, however. If you're planning on taking lots of flights during your adventure, then this site is indispensable, as it has teamed up with airlines Qantas and British Airways to provide a round-the-world planner. This helps you to plot your route using the Discovery Fare. Or, if you don't want to plan your own route, they have lots of existing flight routes in place, such as The Classic, which incorporates Bangkok, Sydney, Aukland, Fiji, Los Angeles and back to the UK, from £721.

One thing to keep an eye one when you're booking flights is taxes. What may seem a bargain can suddenly almost double in price when taxes are added, so be sure to budget for this extra expense. Also be aware that most airlines will charge extra if you go over their weight restrictions, which can be as little as 15kg (33lb) for a tiny aircraft. You don't want to be stung with excess baggage, so try to pack as lightly as possible.

ACCOMMODATION

Some travellers prefer simply to turn up at a destination and seek out somewhere to lay their head. While this is an exciting way to choose your accommodation, it's not recommended for inexperienced travellers or those that like to be in control of situations. The worry of not having a place to stay at night has the potential to ruin some people's travelling experience.

With this in mind, I'd suggest at least hunting out some possible accommodation options before you leave and taking the information with you, or booking in advance.

If you're sticking to a really tight budget, youth hostels are a great option around the world. Have a browse through www.hostelworld.com, which lists more than 20,000 youth hostels in 170 countries around the globe, from as little as a few pounds a night.

Hostels are a great way of meeting other fellow-minded travellers; you have a constant stream of sightseeing (or drinking) buddies on tap. Modern hostels are a far cry from the dingy dorms of the past, many offering Internet access, modern kitchen facilities or canteen and daily breakfast. Don't be put off by the idea of dormitories.

Many do have communal dorms, but also single, twin or even double rooms too, for a little more cash. You will have to expect a shared bathroom though.

Top Travel Tip

If you're considering staying at any of the Hostelling International (www.hihostels.com) rooms, it's a good idea to join the Youth Hostel Association (www.yha.org.uk). For a membership of £16 you get a discount of £3 off per night anywhere in the world.

Another great budget option is a homestay. In the east, these tend to be very basic, cheap and cheerful places, with minimum furniture and a communal eating area. You'll find them littered along the beachside roads throughout countries like Thailand and Indonesia. More like a budget guesthouse than a hotel, they're usually family run and fantastically cheap (from £1.50 per night upwards), but don't expect en suite bathrooms and a chocolate on your pillow at night.

Homestay does seem to have a slightly different meaning depending on which country you're in. Some homestays, particularly in European countries, mean exactly that; you stay with a family and maybe help out with some chores while you're there, such as farm work or babysitting.

Or, if you're looking literally to stay at someone's house, in a non-hotel kind of way, then you could investigate people willing to give up a room for a night or two. A great place to start is www.couchsurfing.com, which has thousands of users signed up in destinations around the world all offering their sofa (or spare room) for a night or two. It's a great concept and a fantastically cheap way of travelling. Bear in mind that while these offers of a place to stay are vetted and rated by users (much like eBay), there is still a risk involved.

Top Travel Tip

It's also possible to bag free food and accommodation, in exchange for a few hours work a day, usually on farms. www.Helpx.net is one of the biggest programmes.

If you're lucky enough to be a homeowner, then there's also the possibility of exchanging your pad for someone else's place. There are a number of home swapping sites like www.home base-hols.com or www.homeexchange.com that allow you to switch your home with someone elsewhere in the world. If you go down this route you're going to have to be prepared for the fact that the house or flat you're going to may not be as swish as your own; also along with the apartment often come other swaps too, like pets or family popping in to say hi!

Another bargain accommodation idea is camping. Not just for festivals, tents can be a cost-effective and fun shelter while you're away. Advances in materials mean that tents are now fabulously light, so you can realistically strap one to the top of a backpack. This is a great investment if you're going somewhere where you're uncertain of what will be on offer; a tent's an easy back-up plan.

In some countries there are loads of designated campsites, such as Hawaii, where you can pitch your tent pretty much anywhere in the national parks and shore line; other destinations are not so generous. Of course you may want to pitch your tent wherever you happen to end up each evening, which is fine if you're somewhere remote, like Thailand's national parks, where you can nestle your tent in some palm trees beside a particularly gorgeous stretch of beach; in other countries camping anywhere isn't tolerated and if you're caught you're likely to be moved on, particularly if it's private land. Where possible, it's a good idea to hunt out the nearest camp spot as there'll be running water, and maybe even showers! Check out www.campingo.com, which is a complete guide, from tent pitches to camper van places, to thousands of sites in more than 71 countries. It also outlines the facilities available, like electric hook ups and washing machines, so is a really useful web address to take with you on your travels.

If you're booking hotels there are some things to consider. The star rating system seems to differ wildly depending on which country you're in. One country's 2-star is another's 4-star, and stars aren't necessarily given by an independent body, it can even be the hotel itself which claims to be a 3-star on its website or literature. With this in mind, it's fine to use the stars as a guide, but don't book on this alone.

The best thing to do for hotel bookings is to use an online comparative site, like www.expedia.co.uk, which will have extremely competitive rates and give you an idea of what's out there and how much you can afford. However, while sites like www.travelsupermarket.com instantly show cheap deals, do be sure to check individual hotel's websites too for a quick price check, as sometimes they can have special offers on.

WEATHER

It's surprising how many travellers forget to check what the weather will be like before they go to a country. People often believe that if they're jetting off to tropical climes there will be guaranteed sunshine, forgetting that many of these verdant countries are so lush and beautiful precisely because they have a solid rainy season.

If it's sunshine you're after, it's also worth remembering that you can have too much of a good thing. Some African countries in the height of summer, just before the rains, can top 45–50°C (104–122°F), which is like living in an oven if you're not used to high temperatures.

Knowing roughly what the seasons will be when you travel is also helpful for your packing. If you're going to be visiting countries during their cold or rainy season, you're going to need very different sorts of clothes than for hot and dry travel. It's easy to be prepared if you know what the climate will be.

Top Travel Tip

Countries' tourist websites should be able to give you an at-a-glance run down of temperatures and rainfall, but you can also consult websites such as www.weatherbase.com or www.worldclimate.com.

INSURANCE

It can seem like an unnecessary expense when you're sat comfortably at home dreaming of white sand beaches and snorkelling in crystal clear lagoons, but insurance is one of the most important aspects of any trip.

Basically, don't travel without insurance. Medical expenses abroad can be eye-wateringly expensive if you aren't covered. Although it's unlikely anything will happen, if you do happen to injure yourself while white-water rafting, for example, knowing that you're covered is massively reassuring.

It's not just medical expenses that are covered. Insurance can also be used for theft, delayed or cancelled flights, legal costs and adventure sports. If you're travelling to more than one place and for a prolonged time, it is probably more economical to get annual insurance.

When you're choosing your package, do make sure that it suits your plans. For example, if you're going to be enjoying winter sports, like snowboarding and skiing while you're away, check that this is included. Most policies allow you to tailor-make, adding things such as water sports or trekking.

Top Travel Tip

If you're travelling within the EU, you can get a European Health Insurance Card (EHIC) for free or reduced emergency care throughout Europe, from the Post Office® or apply online (www.ehic.org.uk). You do still need to have full travel insurance though.

There are lots of places from which to get your insurance. For convenience, you could arrange your insurance through you bank; car insurance companies such as Direct Line and AA offer good rates. There are also websites, such as

www.direct-travel.co.uk, www.atlasdirect.co.uk and www.go
travelinsurance.co.uk. You can even pick travel insurance
when you're shopping at supermarket chains like Tesco, so
there's no excuse for setting off without cover.

ID & DISCOUNT CARDS

The most obvious ID you're going to need is a valid passport.
Sounds obvious, but you'd be amazed at how many people
arrive at the airport with an out-of-date passport. It needs to be
valid for 10 years with at least six months left on it from the date
that you travel.

To apply for a passport or to renew an existing one,
you'll need to apply to the Identity and Passport Service (IPS),
www.ips.gov.uk. If you're applying for your first adult passport
you will no longer be able to use the fast track one-week
service as they may need to interview you as part of the
passport application process. Also, if you are applying for your
first adult passport (aged 16 and over) and have an existing
child passport, you don't have to wait until your child passport
has nearly expired to renew it; however, there must not be any
more than nine months unexpired validity from the old
passport to the new one. You can renew your passport whenever you wish, but you must pay the full fee and no refund can
be given for the unexpired validity in the old passport.

If you are applying for your first passport, you should plan on
allowing more time than in the past to receive your passport as
you will need to attend an interview. It's recommended that
you submit your application six weeks before you need to
travel and not to book any travel arrangements until the new
passport arrives.

You can get hold of an application from the Post Office's
Check & Send outlets (selected Post Office® branches), or fill
in the online application form request on the Home Office

website, www.ips.gov.uk, and a form will be sent in the post. Alternatively, you can call the 24-hour Passport Adviceline on 0300 222 0000.

If you need to renew an existing adult passport, log on to www.ips.gov.uk to find your nearest passport office. You should apply as early as possible as it is more expensive to fast-track an application. You can renew your passport whenever you want and don't have to wait until your passport has expired to renew it.

The IPS says it tries to process applications in around three weeks from when they arrive at their office, however we've all heard the horror stories of holiday makers waiting months for passports. That period doesn't include postage time and applications can take longer at busy times. So, it's best to use the check and send service offered by selected Post Office® branches.

However, if you need to make an urgent application (you need your passport within two weeks) you should call the IPS 24-hour passport line, 0300 222 0000 to make an appointment at your nearest passport office. There's a Fast Track service and a Premium same-day service, which both cost more money than the usual process.

Passports aren't the only form of ID that's handy when you're travelling. If you're a student, The International Student Identity Card (ISIC), which only costs £9, gives you thousands of travel, online and lifestyle discounts. It's accepted worldwide in more than 100 countries including Australia, Brazil, Bulgaria, Costa Rica, Czech Republic, Egypt, Denmark, France, Hong Kong, India, Iran, Italy, Mexico, New Zealand, Peru, Poland, Russia, South Africa, Tanzania and the USA. There are discounts with more than 40,000 businesses, including restaurants, guidebooks, travel gear, hotels, tours, attractions, museums, galleries, audio phrase books, CDs & DVDs, takeaways and even carbon offsetting.

You can lay your hands on an ISIC if you're a full-time student at either a sixth-form or further education college, language school, The Open University (60 points or more), or any UK university. And if you're taking a year out before university and have a deferred or confirmed UCAS placement, you can use an ISIC for your year off.

TRAVEL GUIDES

If you were planning to fix your car or wanted to learn how to draw, chances are you'd buy a book about it, and travel isn't really any different. The saying 'to be forewarned is to be forearmed' is true; if you know about a country and any possible areas of danger or problems, you will know how to handle them and even more importantly, how to avoid them.

This is where guidebooks, or online guides, are so important. It's not just that they can reveal a country to you instantly and easily, saving you a lot of wasted time and energy spent in places that aren't right for you, it's also that they can help to keep you safe, with lots of useful hints and tips.

There can be a degree of snobbery among travellers about guidebooks, but I'd thoroughly recommend reading up about the places that you're going to. For a start you'll appear more knowledgeable to locals, which is always a bonus as they'll think you have an interest in their country. And if you're time-short, guides can help you cut through the rubbish and pin point where you want to be when, and what you want to see and how you can achieve this.

The well-known guides, such as Lonely Planet and Rough Guides are a great starting point, but I'd advise hunting out some of the more specialist titles, such as Bradt guides and Footprint guides, which are really in-depth and pretty unbeatable when it comes to insider knowledge.

Since the Internet revolution, travel guides seem to spring up daily on the web, some more successful than others. World Travel Guide, www.worldtravelguide.net is a great starting point for finding out more about countries and what to see and do, with information on everything from money and duty free, to going out and getting around. Word Travels, www.word travels.com offers a similar service.

Alongside the established guidebooks and websites, written by professional travel writers, there are also the burgeoning blogs and real-life advice from members of the public. The most well-known source is Trip Advisor, www.tripadvisor. co.uk, where members of the public are invited to rate and make comments on hotels, airlines, restaurants, sightseeing and excursions around the world. It's a very useful service, but bear in mind that it's not free from bias, as there's nothing to stop rival hoteliers logging on and badly rating another's accommodation, so I wouldn't advise using this as your only source of research before a trip.

Some of the national newspapers have excellent online travel sites, particularly the award-winning *The Guardian*, www.guardian.co.uk/travel. High-end glossy travel magazine www.cntraveller.co.uk is another good source of information, particularly for in-the-know city advice.

LANGUAGE CLASSES

It can be really rewarding to be able to speak a little of the language of the places that you're visiting. Obviously it will help immediately with the basics, like asking for a hotel room or bus stop, but it also provides a connection to the people that live there that you wouldn't otherwise experience.

If you're heading overseas to improve a language, then you've already taken care of this section. But if you're one of the many jetting off whose only languages are English and a smattering of French phrases, it's well worth taking a bit of time out to teach yourself some more.

There are lots of ways to learn and improve a language, investing in a phrase book is cheap and not that expensive. A useful tip is to put Post-It notes on objects around your house with relevant words on, such as 'computer', so that every time you see that item, you're also seeing the foreign word for it.

You could invest a little more money in a language course. Many books also now come with a DVD of interactive work, which are really effective. There are online courses too, such as the great BBC website, www.bbc.co.uk/languages, which offers excellent 12-week beginner's courses, with video footage, in 36 languages, including Chinese, French, Spanish and Italian. It's completely free, but you do have to have broadband to use the service effectively.

If you're really keen, you could consider enrolling at a language school or night class. They're offered across the country and are a good way of improving quickly as you'll be interacting with other students in real-life situations. Check out your local schools, community centres and colleges for after-hours language classes.

GADGETS

I've heard many pub stories of travellers circumnavigating the globe with just their passport, a Visa card and the clothes they're wearing, but I wouldn't advise it. Why make life hard for yourself? I'm not suggesting you pay thousands of pounds in excess baggage to take your matching Louis Vuitton luggage set, but you can now buy such lightweight gear it's possible to pack a lot without it being a strain.

After years of using heavy suitcases, I was converted to rucksacks after stealing a friend's for a particularly adventurous trip to the mountainous Musandam Peninsula in Oman.

I haven't found anything better than a rucksack to transport a lot of things around efficiently and easily. A suitcase is a pain to lug around with you if you're visiting several places, it becomes heavy to carry and is easier to lose or be stolen – a rucksack is strapped to your back.

A rucksack of soft material can also double up as a pillow on which to lay your head if you luck-out on accommodation on the occasional night. It's also great to lean against if you're having to queue, and it's also like Doctor Who's Tardis as it can seemingly hold much, much more than you would at first guess.

A rucksack is also really handy for attaching things to. Everything from torches to cups and sleeping bags can be tied onto your faithful rucksack, which makes it like a mini mobile home.

So, what to fill you rucksack with? Apart from the obvious, your clothes, there are loads of excellent travel gear and gadgets to take along that won't weigh a ton. My most recent find is insect repellent clothing. Also, if you can squeeze in a mosquito net it's well worth doing, particularly if you're travelling to a country with deadly strains of malaria and are going to be staying in basic accommodation.

Top Travel Tip

A head torch is really useful as it allows you to use both hands in the pitch dark. You might not think you're going to need such a thing, but you'll find it indispensable if you're pitching a tent or finding a loo!

Antibacterial hand gel is a good investment to use for things like unhygienic toilets without running water, or before eating food with your hands. I'd also recommend a wind-up torch.

These now last up to half an hour, you don't have to be a body builder to wind it up and you never know when you're going to be able to buy batteries; so it's less of a headache than a normal torch, plus the eco choice.

Invest in dry bags (waterproof pouches) if you're going to be diving, snorkelling or doing any water-based sports where you don't want to leave valuables unattended. A fold-up washbag, which will easily hold all your toiletries and has a hook so can be hung up, is a worthwhile investment, too.

A whistle is always a good idea, for alerting attention and also for warding off unwanted attention, and a multi-tool, like a traditional Swiss Army knife, with scissors, corkscrew, knife, bottle opener, screwdriver, hook and tweezers is invaluable.

A small first-aid kit should not be left out, no matter how full your rucksack. This should include, at a very minimum, dressing, plasters, antiseptic cream, burn-gel, bandage, eye pad, vinyl gloves, paracetamol and anti-diarrhoea tablets.

Checklist

* Set a budget ☑
* Start saving ☑
* Use the Internet for research ☑
* Book flights ☑
* Find accommodation ☑
* Check the weather ☑
* Get travel insurance ☑
* Investigate ID and discount cards ☑
* Check out travel guides ☑
* Learn a bit of the language ☑
* Invest in a rucksack ☑
* Buy gadgets ☑

Chapter 3
Solo travel

Solo travelling is an incredibly exciting prospect, but also rather daunting. It can make you feel really intrepid and brave, can certainly be a confidence booster and even life-changing. But as you'd expect, solo adventures also mean you do have to be extra cautious and super organised, as there's no one else to rely on.

If you're going to travel alone, the good news is that you're not alone (so to speak)! There's been a huge rise in the number of single travellers in recent years, particularly female; around 45 per cent of solo travellers are now women. More and more people are taking off on their own to discover the world and certainly don't feel that they have to wait around for a partner or a mate to get their act together. Consequently many countries are more geared towards solos and less shocked at the sight of a female travelling alone.

PROS & CONS

If you're still deliberating about whether to travel alone, it's worth weighing up the pros and cons. One of the major pluses is that you don't have to compromise. We've all been away with someone who has a very different idea of what makes a great trip – they want to lie on a beach for two months, you want to trek to Machu Picchu. If you're travelling by yourself you can go where you want, when you want, and if you've never had that luxury before let me assure you, it's fantastic. Going solo allows you to travel in a way that is completely different to being with someone else, whether you want to try a local restaurant (no worrying about another person's weird food allergies) or sleep in a hammock for a day, you can without anyone nagging you.

It's also great not to have the inevitable money worries or rows that couples or groups of friends sometimes have when travelling. You won't have the headache of who pays for what, kitties and who's broke and can't afford to fly home; instead it's just you and your cash card, which is much easier to manage.

The other great thing about solo travel in my experience is that, far from making you feel alone, it can actually end up being an incredibly social experience. You often meet more people precisely because you're alone. If you're travelling around countries, you're constantly meeting new people and they're more likely to start chatting to you if you're alone, than say if you're with a partner.

If you're single and looking for love, or at least someone to cosy up with, then single travel is a fantastic way to meet new and interesting potential hook ups, with the added bonus that you can move on to another country if it turns pear shaped. If you're currently going through a dating drought, you'll be amazed at how travel can open up your eyes to how many other singles are out there and how experiences can bring you together. The other bonuses are that, in another country, you'll stand out and you don't have any of the pressure that friends can put on you. If you like someone, you can go for it without feeling embarrassed; after all, no one back home is going to know if you're rejected.

That's not to say that there aren't down sides to heading out alone. For many people the idea of not having someone to share experiences with is off-putting, as is the thought of not having a mate alongside you in case of emergencies or to help sort out problems. Many people worry that they'll end up feeling lonely and not meet any likeminded travellers, which will be detrimental to their time away. If this is how you're feeling, the best advice is to have a trial run. Book yourself a long weekend or week away somewhere and see how you get on.

Top Travel Tip

Another downside to solo travel, if you're not careful, is that many tour operators, hotels and ships will charge a large supplement for a single room. It's unfair, but lots of places do charge extra, so be sure to check this before you book.

SOLO SAFTEY

You've chosen to go it alone and you're looking forward to having the time of your life. However, you're going to have to take precautions to make sure that you stay safe and can look after yourself in a crisis.

Theft and muggings are a sad fact of life when you're travelling. It may not happen to you, but you'll hear stories wherever you go about people who have had things stolen from their money to their passport. Recent statistics allege that a British tourist is robbed every 31 seconds, which stacks up to one million people per year. Unfortunately, lone travellers are often seen as easier pickings. There isn't anyone to watch your belongings if you nip to the loo, and it's simpler to carry out a distraction theft on one rather than two people. With this in mind, it's vital that you're aware of the dangers and keep your valuables close to you at all times.

Using a pre-paid money card or credit card rather than carrying large amounts of cash around is sound advice, as you can stop transactions being made. Check out Post Office® Travel Money Card (www.postoffice.co.uk) which can be used in most countries and anywhere that the Visa sign is found.

Top Travel Tip

Be sure to take emergency banking telephone numbers away with you so you can cancel your cards quickly at any time.

Sticking to streets where there are other people is always wise, and carrying a duplicate, empty purse or wallet is an old trick – you can hand it over if threatened, and won't worry if it's pickpocketed. If you're planning to put all of your possessions in a rucksack, think again; as they're out of your eye view, backpacks are quite easy to take from. If you're considering putting your money and other valuables in a long-strap bag worn across the chest or over the shoulder, reconsider, as they are a target for thieves on the move, such as on bikes or mopeds, as they're easy to grab hold of and drag off you. Instead, put all your valuables closer to home. Wearing a money belt – not a bum bag, which clips on to your belt and is on show – but one which fits beneath your skirt or trouser top so is virtually impossible to steal. When you have to take your bags off, always hold them or place them on the ground beneath your feet. Don't leave them unattended.

Drinking a lot of alcohol can make you much more vulnerable when you're travelling alone. If you're having drinks with strangers that you've just met, it's not advisable to put yourself at risk by becoming heavily intoxicated, even if they seem like great people. If you're in a strange country where you don't know the language, people aren't looking out for you and you're drunk. In short you're an easy target, be it theft or rape. One of the major drawbacks of alcohol is that it can impair your memory – most people have woken up the morning after the night before knowing that they got up to something but not quite sure what. That can be funny if you've been out with friends and are in your safety zone; it can be terrifying if you're on your own and have no idea where you are. In the worst case scenario, it also makes your evidence less conclusive to police if you need to report a crime.

It's worth taking a self-defence course before you go away. It's unlikely that you'd need to use anything that you learnt, but the confidence that knowing you can handle yourself brings is worth its weight in gold. Not looking vulnerable, and acting with confidence gives you the sort of body language that's likely to make you less of a potential target for any sort of attack.

One of the downsides of solo female travel can be the unwanted attention of men. Depending on which country you're travelling in, the fact the you're alone can create any-thing from mild curiosity to full-on harassment. While most women are used to handling a bit of male attention, it can be a bit overwhelming if it's a constant flow of questions and gestures wherever you go, so to avoid unwanted attention, here are some tips. If you're in a country with particularly macho attitudes towards women, or where solo female travel is unusual, it can help matters by popping a ring on your wedding finger. Also carry a picture of a relative or friend's child and pretend that it's yours, as you're more likely to receive a respectful attitude if you're a mother and wife. In male-dominated Muslim countries, such as parts of the Middle East and Africa, Pakistan, some areas of India and Latin America, it's a good idea to avoid skimpy shorts and skirts, and to follow the local women's lead; if they cover their shoulders and legs, then you should too to blend in. You may not be aware, but smoking, drinking and even wearing make-up is the sign of a 'loose' woman in some countries, so be careful when you're socialising. With men that you've never met before, be polite, but not overly friendly as this may be misinterpreted, and if you're being harassed, by whispering or groping, the best action is to ignore it and walk confidently away. If, however, you become scared in a situation, speak very assertively (even if you're quivering inside), shouting if necessary, telling them to leave you alone and back off.

Travelling can make you feel wonderfully alive and adventurous, and the inevitable consequence of that feeling is that you sometimes end up doing things that you wouldn't dream of at home. Hitch-hiking is a good example. It's unlikely that you'd stand on the side of the road of the M1 motorway at 11pm in the UK as it's dangerous, but somehow what's risky in one country can seem fun and exciting, particularly in a hot destination where everyone seems friendly and you don't have much cash. I'd advise against hitch-hiking if you're travelling alone, but if this is your plan for transport, then make sure you read up on safety in the countries you're travelling to – if crime rates are high, then think again. Also, make sure your mobile phone is charged and easy to get to, start your hitch-hiking at a place with CCTV cameras, such as a petrol station, and always make a note of the vehicle registration.

You should also be aware of drug smuggling when you're a solo traveller, as you're more vulnerable than if you're with friends or a partner. At friendly UK airports we often laugh when we're asked if we packed our bags ourselves or are carrying anything illegal, but it's actually vitally important that you do pack your rucksack yourself and check that nothing has been planted in there.

In addition, never, ever agree to carry bags or packages for someone else. You may think this isn't advice worth taking on board as it's so unlikely, but you'd be surprised how many foreigners get suckered into this type of trafficking every year, particularly if you're on your own and have been befriended by someone for a number of months. A request to take a gift to a friend in another country on a backpacker trail can seem all too innocent when you're chilled out and living in very different circumstances to normal.

Money, which is usually on the light side when you're a traveller, can be a real lure. If you're down to your last pennies and don't have a friend at hand to ask for a loan, it might be tempting to make a little extra by dabbling in drugs sales, such as an ounce or two of marijuana to fellow backpackers. Others may offer to pay you considerable sums for package delivery, but it must be stressed that this kind of action just isn't worth it. If you're out of cash, go home rather than risk wasting 20 years of your life in prison – after all, you'll have the chance to travel again at some point.

SOLO SOCIALISING

One of the big dreads for many people when it comes to travelling alone is the idea of not having anyone to socialise with. It's okay to sightsee and travel alone, but going out can be a different matter, as lots of people don't want to eat and drink by themselves.

This is perfectly understandable, as it can be lonely if you're in what is considered to be a happening destination, where everyone around you appears to be partying, and you're haven't got someone to go out on the town with. However, there are lots of tips for making sure that solo travellers get the best out of a place too.

Research and organisation is key to most areas of travel and this is true of single socialising too. Rather than just rolling up to a resort or city without having a clue about the place, find out online what's going to be on while you're there and throw yourself into it. Whether it's a festival, music gig, football match or speed-dating night, there's going to be something fun on that you can take part in with other members of the public.

Being able to exchange a few words of a local language is an excellent way to open doors. Outside of Europe, people are usually impressed if you've bothered to learn some of their language before visiting their country so you'll make a good impression. Luckily, English is widely spoken throughout the world, so unless you're somewhere incredibly remote, it's unlikely you'll have to travel far before you meet someone you can have a conversation with.

Be mindful of different cultures; what's acceptable in one country may be frowned upon in another. For example, if you're in a strict Muslim country, it's advisable to cover your shoulders, legs and head and not to drink; if you're in central or Southeast Asia, don't pass food or eat it with your left hand, as that's considered rude as it's traditionally the hand used in the absence of toilet paper. Research as much as you can before you go, as you don't want to offend people through ignorance.

Top Travel Tip

The website www.travellingalone.co.uk has lots of useful advice on solo travel, particularly safety and planning.

If you are female and want to start off solo but meet up with people along the way so that you do share some experiences, then check out a fantastic website called www.thelmaand louise.com dedicated to helping likeminded women travellers get together. There are members of the Thelma & Louise Club all over the world, so you can get in contact with them to let them know you'll be visiting their city or country and get a guided tour. Other members are looking for a travelling companion for certain stages of their travel, such as a trek.

GROUP TRIPS FOR SOLOS

If you're on your own but would rather not travel alone, the answer could be a group trip for singles. There are lots on the market, from cooking holidays to trekking in Nepal, so it's likely you'll be able to find one to match your needs.

The benefits are numerous. For a start you're probably going to go away with likeminded people, who are also seeking adventure and looking for sociability. Having a trained guide with you can really take the pressure off the scary aspects of travelling alone, and sharing the costs for things will help your money go further. If you're worried about hanging out with total strangers, then bear in mind that if it's an activity-based trip, there's always going to be something exciting happening each day to distract you if you aren't getting on with all of your fellow travellers.

If you're looking for out and out adventure, www.explore. co.uk and www.intrepidtravel.com both offer really excellent group trips, including Polar expeditions, African adventures and Middle Eastern holidays. In Australia and New Zealand, OzXposure (www.letstrekaustralia.com) allows you to join up with other singles while you're on the continent to enjoy all kinds of amazing experiences, from reef and rainforest to bush camps and volcano trails. American Adventures (www.trek america.com) offers the same sort of service in the USA. It particularly prides itself on being North America's 18 to 38s specialist for off-the-beaten-track adventure travel as well as offering jaunts to Mexico and Alaska. Plus it guarantees no single supplements.

Checklist

* Consider pre-paid money cards ☑
* Buy a money belt ☑
* Take a self-defence course ☑
* Find out what social events are on at
  your destination online prior to travel ☑
* Find out about a country's culture before
  travel ☑
* Check out group trips/solo travel websites ☑

Chapter 4
Gap years

It's become the norm to take a year out travelling before starting college or university or even during the course, but increasingly people are also taking gap years at other times in their life and reaping the benefits. A year-break can do wonders for your confidence, skills and CV.

GAP YEAR OPTIONS

You've got a free 12 months stretching out ahead of you and nothing planned, how are you going to fill it? The options for gap years seem to multiply and become more exciting each year, with more and more companies and destinations geared towards making sure you have the time of your life while you're away. Many gappers opt for the adventure travel option, filling their year with action-packed experiences mixed in with some beach action. This is a great way of getting to see the world, meeting likeminded travellers and having memories that will last a lifetime.

However, a year of adventure travel isn't your only option, there are lots of great ways to spend your year. You may decide you want to spend only part of your time travelling and some of it back in the UK working or volunteering – this is particularly relevant if you only have a small budget. Don't think that just because your mates are going away for 12 months, you have to stretch your resources and do the same; it's not a necessity and it's crazy to go into lots of debt before you even start your studies. Remember you can always spend time travelling at the end of your studies or during a work sabbatical.

Some people want to get more out of their time away than just adventure activities. For instance, a gap year could be a time to study. Okay, if you're a student you may be thinking that you want to forget study for a while and concentrate on the fun side of life. But there's nothing to stop you, on your year off, learning a skill that you've always wanted to and making it an exciting and enjoyable experience, such as learning Spanish in Costa Rica or salsa dancing in Argentina.

Many gap year travellers decide they want to make a contribution to a community abroad and volunteer for some or all of their time overseas. Voluntary work can be very rewarding, although the same factors, which can limit the value of gap years generally, such as language and cultural barriers, apply here too. Volunteering projects require careful structuring, planning and support, and volunteers will get more benefit the longer the project and the closer it matches their skills. For more information on volunteer holidays see Chapter 5.

Working while you travel is a great way to help finance your trip, allowing you to stay away for longer. If you are planning to earn a bit of extra cash abroad, make sure you have the correct work permit and visas. Also ensure you properly check out any potential employer before your interview and let friends or family know where you are going and who you are meeting. For more information on working abroad see Chapter 8.

GAP YEAR COMPANIES

There are loads of companies on the market geared up to making sure you have the time of your life, but inevitably there are also some dodgy ones just waiting to take your money.

With this in mind, do your research very carefully before committing.

Before you part with any cash, find out a few essentials like how long they have been operating and how many people they have taken abroad in the past. If the company has a website with a forum, it's worth putting up a post to ask if people would recommend the company, though you can usually tell from what's been written whether it's a popular operation. It's also a good idea to speak to past gap travellers for company recommendations.

Top Travel Tip

Find out if the company is a member of ABTA (Association of British Tour Operators) as this will ensure industry standards and also help with insurance in the event of a company going under.

There are hundreds of companies fighting for your custom, but for all-round experiences, with a huge amount of trips on offer for various lengths of time, www.globalxperience.com is a great place to start. It helps you to plot your route and what experiences you'd like to include along the way, plus allows lots of flexibility so you don't have to feel like your year is set in stone. Ditto www.gapyear.com, which is very comprehensive, provides lots of ideas and has a really active membership forum so you can ask lots of questions and get unbiased answers. There's also a gap year eZine you can sign up to, and even a travel-buddy finding service if you're after company while you're roaming. Also check out www.realgap.co.uk and www.gapwork.com.

PLANNING YOUR GAP YEAR

If you're keen on the idea of planning your own year away, then it's going to take a bit of research as you want to make sure that you get the most you can for your money. Don't just book the first thing you find on a whim, think seriously about where you've always wanted to travel to and find out whether these destinations are easy to transfer between. If you don't have a clue about where you want to go, take a look at the most popular routes for inspiration, which are detailed later in this chapter.

Flights are one of the biggest expenses of any gap year. Many gappers decide to go for a Round the World ticket (RTW), which is a series of single flights on one ticket, as mentioned earlier. They're usually valid for 12 months and incorporate Australia and allow you to build your own route. The most popular route, according to www.gapyear.com is London, LA, Fiji, Cook Islands, New Zealand, Australia, Singapore, Thailand, London. The beauty of this flexible air ticket is that you know 100 per cent that you can come home or leave a country whenever you want without being restricted. The good news is that the prices aren't as eye watering as you'd expect. A basic 4–6 stop route starting mid-season (Sept, Oct, Jan and March) comes in at around £1,500 to £1,800, although you can get them cheaper if you travel off-peak.

Top Travel Tip

If you're an inexperienced traveller, book a round-the-world trip west to east, as Southeast Asia can be a bit full-on if it's the first place that you land, but by the time you get there after touring Australia you'll be an old hand.

Of course there are lots of other route combinations available. Other popular routes include India, Australia and South America, or even a route called The Edge of the Earth and Back, which takes in Reykjavik, Toronto, Miami, Lima, Buenos Aires, Auckland, Shanghai, Bangkok and Bahrain.

Top Travel Tip

For easy route planning and the top five RTW flight itineraries, check out www.statravel.co.uk, which is the authority on student travel and offers pretty much every service you could require for your gap year.

When you've sorted out your flights, you can concentrate on the finer details, like travel while you're in a destination. If you've just landed in a new destination, it's good to know your transport options in advance, particularly in a country where there may be language difficulties. It's all too easy to be fleeced by unscrupulous taxis and bus companies. Rail is a fantastic way of getting around a country quickly, easily, efficiently and most of all, cheaply.

If you're planning to travel around Europe in your gap year, then it's worth investing in an InterRail Global Pass (www.interrail.net), which allows you to travel to up to 30 countries in a month. It's fantastic value for money and really flexible, and costs around £550 second class. In Australia, the Austrail Flexi Pass gives unlimited and flexible train travel on Rail Australia for 15 to 22 days within six months, and costs around £450 (www.railaustralia.com.au). Japan is exceedingly well set up for rail travel, with its futuristic bullet trains, and the Japan Rail Pass offers unlimited travel on all lines, affiliated buses and ferries for up to 21 days (www.japanrailpass.net).

India has Indrail, which is a brilliant budget way to explore this vast continent (www.indianrail.gov.in). There's no route restriction and you can get a pass from half a day (around £30) to 90 days (more than £500). In gap year favourite Thailand, rail is by far the best form of transport, and fantastic value for money (www.thailandbytrain.com). You can take a train from Bangkok to Penang, Kuala Lumpur and Singapore from just £33 one-way – that's 1,249 miles (2,010km)!

Top Travel Tip

The best source I've discovered for international rail and ferry information and booking is www.seat 61.com, which provides everything from fares and timetables in countries all over the world to the latest news and advice.

Bus is another obvious form of cheap transport, with the added bonus that there are often more stops and options than rail travel. The downside is that it can be very slow, but the plus side is that if you get a window seat it's a wonderful way of viewing a country. Some countries offer a Hop on, Hop off service, allowing you to buy a ticket for unlimited journeys, with complete flexibility.

Gap year accommodation is a tricky one, as most travellers don't want to book in advance as they want the flexibility of moving on as and when they feel like it. That's fine, but it's good to do some research before you land in a destination so that you at least have the contact details of a couple of hostels, homestays or hotels in the area. Otherwise you might end up homeless or paying a fortune for your first night. You'll find that when you're on the gap year trail, you'll find out some great places through word of mouth; other gappers that you bump into will be able to recommend some places and tell you which ones to avoid.

SABBATICALS

If you're in full-time work and reading this book for fantasy or ideas on what you can do when you eventually manage to escape the 9–5, then heading off to foreign climes for a long period is much harder and more complicated.

It's likely that, if you're full time, you get around four to five weeks holiday per year, more in jobs such as teaching. As pointed out in Chapter 9 on shorter trips, it's perfectly possible to head off and have a fantastic travelling experience in less than a month. However, if you feel the time has come for a prolonged leave, read on.

What is a sabbatical?

A sabbatical is an agreed period of leave (usually from three months to one year) from your employment, which guarantees that your job will still be yours when you return. In short, your employer will give you time off work (paid or unpaid) in addition to your usual holiday allowance.

Sound good? Yes it does, however not all employers offer this as an option and even if they do, you may have to have worked there for a specified amount of time, such as 10 years. Companies offering sabbaticals do vary wildly. For example, *The Guardian* newspaper allows employees to take a month off on full pay every four years and the Royal College of Nursing lets staff take two months sabbatical every five years, after six years' initial service.

Do I qualify for a sabbatical?

Your first step, if you're really set on the idea of an extended break, is to find out if your employer has any regulations in place. If you're in a large corporation, get in touch with the Human Resources or Personnel department as a first port of call as they'll be able to provide you with a low down without your boss knowing you want a break. Sabbaticals aren't always widely publicised in companies, for obvious reasons, so you may be pleasantly surprised.

If you're in a smaller place of work, ask some trusted colleagues whether anyone has ever taken a sabbatical, so you're armed with the knowledge before you approach your boss to discuss the matter.

Luckily, the concept of offering a sabbatical has become increasingly popular amongst companies and employers because of the fact that such a high percentage of people these days opt for a career break at some point. By allowing their staff to take a sabbatical companies benefit because they are not losing valuable employees in the long term.

The next step is to approach your boss to request your sabbatical. If a procedure is in place, and you don't fulfil the criteria – such as you haven't been at the company for a stipulated amount of time – then it's unlikely you're going to get very far. However, if you meet the guidelines or there has been a precedent of sabbaticals, then you're certainly in with a chance.

Top Travel Tip

If your employer doesn't already have a sabbatical scheme set in place, it's perfectly acceptable for you to suggest one, making clear the benefits for both sides. The worst thing they can do is say no!

The most important thing before you present your argument to your employer is to do plenty of research and think about how you can persuade them that your heading off for three or six months is a great idea.

In all scenarios, you need to be armed with examples of companies that offer sabbaticals to their employees. Point out that many firms offer career breaks because it's a great reward for a long period of service in a market place where staff are often moving jobs after less than 18 months. It allegedly now costs around £8,000 to employ a new member of staff, from adverts to lost work time due to interviews, so the fact that you want to return to your place of work after your time away should be highlighted (and a good reason for them to let you go!).

One of the major arguments you can use is that you would be willing to develop skills while you're away to improve your performance when you're back at work. This doesn't mean you have to give up your dream of touring various parts of the world, but it's worth investigating schemes that are useful for work too. If you're in management, find volunteering schemes which involve you being in charge of a team and challenging budget, if you're a teacher, you could opt for teaching in a foreign language which will benefit your own students on your return.

Preparing for a sabbatical

The vast majority of sabbaticals are unpaid, so you need to bear this in mind – can you afford no income for six months? If you've got the green light from your work place, the best plan of action is not to take out a loan and head off. If you can wait and save up enough money to cover you while you're away, do it. One of the reasons many people want a career break is because they're stressed and feel overworked. Constantly worrying about cash while you're away will not help you to come back refreshed and ready for work again. Set up a special bank account just for your trip, make it a high interest one which you're not allowed to touch and set up a direct debit from your current account – you'll be amazed how quickly it builds up.

Also, set out goals and the exact amount of time you're planning to take off. It may not sound spontaneous and exciting, but it's really important so you can approximate what the whole thing is going to cost. If you're planning on doing some volunteering work followed by adventure travel, build these into your budget.

Plus, you'll need to be aware of costs back home. I know it sounds obvious, but it's easy to forget that bills are still going to be arriving through your letterbox while you're away. If you haven't already, get as much transferred to direct debit as possible, so you know what's going out when. If you're worried about paying a mortgage, then consider getting a lodger in to cover the period you'll be away. There are lots of websites to help with this, such as www.sublet.com, which offer short-term housing lets around the world.

If the sabbatical involves taking a temporary job, there's a chance it will include health-care coverage. Otherwise, you are facing a substantial out-of-pocket expense. One option is to take out a health insurance policy with a high deductible and relatively low monthly premium to preserve cash flow. However, when maintaining the most comprehensive coverage is the goal, staying with an employer's plan may be the best alternative.

Be prepared that you may have such a wonderful time, it may lead you not to return to your original type of work. This is a really common reaction, so don't despair if it happens to you. However, do think carefully before jacking everything in! Think about what it is that you really want to do. Could you make your job more rewarding using skills that you've learnt from your placement? Is it the job or the fact that you were working overseas?

Top Travel Tip

For more sabbatical ideas, take a look at www.gapyearforgrownups.co.uk/sabbatical.

WHAT TO DO?

Use this book as inspiration as to what you could do during your time out from work. Volunteering is a wonderfully fulfilling experience which can provide you with that much needed break you were after, the chance to travel and a new outlook on life. To make the best of your time it might be an idea to combine volunteer work with some travelling the world, visiting places you've always wanted to see. This combination should keep you and your employer happy.

If you're feeling like you really need to change your lifestyle, and possibly even your job, then take a look at Chapter 12, on life changing travel. From holistic retreats to learning a new skill, this sort of travel experience could be just what you need to get back on track.

TOP 10 GAP YEAR DESTINATIONS

There are some destinations which stand out for gap year adventures. From great weather to jaw-dropping landscapes and fantastic value for money, they particularly appeal to young travellers. Here are 10 popular destinations to get you started which are guaranteed to give you itchy feet.

Thailand

Thailand has been a magnet for gappers for years. Flights to Bangkok are frequent and relatively cheap, and from there it's easy to reach the fun beach resorts of Phuket and Krabi. The islands off Thailand's southern shores are particularly beautiful and popular with backpackers, like Koh Phi Phi. Koh Samui is known for its full moon parties and nightlife. There's also jungle to explore in Khao Sok National Park, and it's easy to move on to Malaysia.

Goa

Goa is also a popular haven for people on their gap year. India's laid-back province is home to the hippy scene at Kerala, which also boasts golden beaches, bustling Chennai city which has a burgeoning arts and music scene, and the amazing shore temples of Mamallapuram. It's also really, really cheap, so can you stay here for a long time without breaking the bank.

Australia

Australia is a natural choice for those new to travelling as it offers all of the excitement of off-the-beaten-track adventure, but there's no language barrier and it is relatively hassle-free compared to exploring the Third World. The Gold Coast in Queensland is legendary, thanks to the glitz of Cairns, the white sand beaches, surfing action and proximity to the Great Barrier Reef. The interior, from bush treks to jungle exploration, is equally as exciting.

Borneo

Borneo makes it onto the list for many, who are drawn by experiences like climbing Mount Kinabalu, trekking through rainforest (although that's disappearing at an alarming rate), hanging out in tribal villages, meeting orangutans and enjoying local hospitality and incredibly cheap homestays.

Costa Rica

South American country is a top stop for nature lovers on a gap year, as it offers greater biodiversity than Europe or North America. There's rainforest to explore, with an abundance of wildlife to discover, pristine beaches to relax on, hot springs to jump in and all manner of adventure activities, from white-water rafting to climbing an active volcano.

Peru

Peru, also in South America, is immensely popular – particularly treks to places like Machu Picchu and Lake Titicaca. The untouched Santa Cruz Valley is unmissable, as is a trip along the Amazon – white-water rafting, or at a more leisurely pace.

South Africa

This destination regularly tops list of gap year favourites because, like Australia, there's so much to do. It's an enormous country, stretching 2,000km (1,250 miles) from north to south, offering the chance to track some of the world's most exciting wildlife, from lions to elephants, on safari; there's also mountain climbing, ancient tribes and their customs, some of the world's best surfing and chilling out in super cool Cape Town.

New Zealand

New Zealand is an increasingly desirable stop-off on a round-the-world trip; it's relatively crime free, there's no language barrier, it's fantastically remote and offers pretty much any outdoor pursuit you can think of, from mountaineering and trekking to bungee jumping and horse riding. Oh, and the landscape (as featured in the *Lord of the Rings* films) is incredible.

Tanzania

A wildly exotic part of Africa, Tanzania appeals to those seeking to get away from the norm. The top attraction here is climbing snow-peaked Mount Kilimanjaro, the world's highest free-standing mountain, which takes at least five days to summit. Other lures include superb safaris and the islands of Pemba and Zanzibar.

Canada

Canada is a great option for those wanting to head west on their adventure. It's the second-largest country in the world, so there's a hell of a lot on offer and some gappers end up spending a whole year exploring it. Canada's scenery and wildlife are its biggest draw and its ski and snowboarding resorts in the Rocky Mountains are magical. There are 3,000km (1,875 miles) of walking trails in the Rockies so it's equally as inspiring in the summer. Vancouver city provides a nightlife hit.

MONEY MATTERS

Okay, now it's the boring bit. You've planned your dream trip, but you need to make sure your finances are in order and your money safe while you're away.

The first serious point to consider is do you have enough money to take a gap year? It sounds ridiculous, but you'd be amazed at how many people just book and hope, with no real idea of how they're ever going to pay for their trip. If you're taking a gap year before university and don't have funds saved up, it's possible to get a loan. But bear in mind that it's highly likely you're going to rack up a big student loan during your studies – do you really want to start your student days already in debt? If the answer's yes, then no worries, but if you don't fancy going into the red before you've even opened a textbook, then you might have to think about either working your way around the world or getting a job and working for six months to pay for the next six months of travel.

You can be creative when it comes to raising funds for your gap year. If you're a student-to-be, is there anything you can sell? For example a car may have been invaluable to you when you were 17, but most universities are based in city centres or close by, with excellent transport links, so do you really need a vehicle? If you're taking a gap year in your 20s or 30s, then set up a high-interest account and get saving.

Once you've got your money in place, you're going to need to set budget. If you do your research, it's fairly easy to guesstimate the amount you'll spend on flights, overground transport, accommodation, food and extras, such as adventure activities. I met a girl at university who told me she had exactly £1 left in her account after a year of travelling, she'd budgeted so accurately. Not many people are that precise, or disciplined, but you do need to make sure you have enough to cover you while you're away. So take time to plan how much you have to spend each day or at least each week.

When everything is in place – your bank account is bulging (ish) and you've booked your flights – it's time to get down to the fundamentals of travelling with money. The first thing is to check the validity, expiry dates and cash available on your credit or debit cards well ahead of your trip; this way you won't have any heart sinking moments or confusing and annoying phone calls across the world. Also, it's best to know your spending limits before they run out.

Due to ever increasing incidences of fraud throughout the world, I'm finding more and more that my card is being blocked by my bank when I try to use my debit card at an ATM or shop when I'm travelling. This is particularly true if you're visiting a country with problem spots, most recently for me Sri Lanka. Having your card blocked can be a real pain if you're in real need of cash, so to prevent this occurring, tell your bank where you're going to be travelling. Also check with them prior to going abroad whether you can use your debit/credit card in the countries you are visiting and whether any card usage charges may apply.

If you're going to be using cards as your main form of payment while you're away, it's essential to keep them safe and with you at all times. My tip is to take at least two cards, but saving one for emergencies only (make sure you know the PINs for both cards and keep them separately). As well as cards, it's worth taking some back-up options, like a few traveller's cheques or even some cash, like Sterling or US dollars, which are exchangeable the world over. If you do take traveller's cheques, make a note of the cheque numbers and the emergency telephone number for them in case they get lost or stolen.

Top Travel Tip

It's advisable to have some local currency in small bank notes so you can easily catch a taxi, give a tip, or get something to eat or drink on arrival.

If you're away for a year, don't forget about money matters in the UK, too. Before you jet off, make sure you've made arrangements for any credit card, household or extra bills to be paid if they aren't on direct debit. Finally, a former gap year traveller gave me a great tip – try and save a little bit of money for when you get home. Getting back from a round-the-world adventure of a lifetime can be incredibly depressing anyway, let alone if you don't have enough money to go for a drink at the pub or buy a meal when you get home.

GAP YEAR TOP TIPS

These tips may seem obvious, but you'd be amazed how many times people get caught out while they're away.

Documentation

Firstly, ensure that you have the necessary visas to travel to your destination. Yes this can take time and money, but you don't want to end up stranded at an airport unable to continue your adventure. Check that your passport is in good condition and make sure you fill in the emergency contact details. Certain countries require you to have a minimum period of time left on your passport when you arrive, which is usually six months – when you're going away for a year this is really important as you won't be able to visit a passport office for renewal. To find out if there is a minimum requirement where you are going, check the FCO's country travel advice at www.fco.gov.uk/travel.

Plan ahead

Flying into a new country without a clue where you're going to stay is putting yourself at risk. At the very least, make sure you have booked your first night's accommodation in advance. You are at your most vulnerable when you first arrive in a foreign country. You are likely to be tired and unsure of your surroundings – so it's worth planning ahead.

Research

Get a good guidebook and carry out a bit of research into your destination before you go, including its laws, customs and language. This will help you avoid offending people or breaking local laws, however unwittingly.

Be money wise

If your money, passport or anything else is stolen abroad, report it to the local police immediately and get a statement about the loss (you will need one to claim against your insurance). You will need to cancel any credit cards or traveller's cheques. You may also want to have money transferred to you either by your bank or by a relative using a reliable money transfer company.

Return air fare

Make sure you have a return air ticket, or enough money to buy one. It's worth noting that if you don't have a return ticket, many countries will refuse you entry unless you can prove you have enough money to buy one. Also be aware that British consular staff can't send you home for free if you run out of money!

LOCATE

Sign up to the Foreign & Commonwealth Office's LOCATE service so that the British Embassy knows where you are in the event of a crisis like a tsunami or a terrorist attack. Information about LOCATE and the registration form can be found at www.fco.gov.uk/locate.

Top Travel Tip

For indispensable free gap year advice and to talk online to other gappers, log on to www.gogapyear.com.

Checklist

* Consider pre-paid money cards ☑
* Investigate gap year companies ☑
* Plan your gap year ☑
* Book flights/other transport ☑
* Set a budget ☑
* Arrange money back-up solutions ☑
* Find out if you need visas ☑
* Is your passport up-to-date with
  enough time left? ☑
* Check out accommodation options
  prior to travel ☑
* Sign up for LOCATE ☑

Chapter 5
Volunteering

If you want to pack your conscience along with your flip-flops, then you should consider volunteer work while you're on your travels. Helping hand holidays are not only fulfilling, they're also a fantastic way of really getting to experience a country below the tourist radar.

WHY VOLUNTEER?

One of the best reasons (if not the most worthy!) for volunteering abroad is that it's a really cheap way of seeing the world. Even though you usually have to pay a sum towards the costs of a project, it's a really budget way of seeing the world, particularly if you can raise money to help pay for it (see fundraising section in this chapter).

Another top reason to volunteer during your time away is that you can experience total immersion in a country's culture, rather than just touching the surface as you pass through. Some locals, and other volunteers, that you'll meet while away will remain lifetime friends; the bond of working together for a considerable length of time is likely to be so much stronger than that with passing travellers lying around on a beach (though that can be great fun too of course!).

There's no denying that helping others really does make you feel better about yourself, so if it's a confidence or self-esteem boost you're after, a stint of volunteering can work wonders. Women's magazines like *Cosmopolitan* often run features about how lending a hand can increase your happiness levels, and they're not wrong. It can also be comforting for some travellers to have a focus. A specific volunteer programme gives you a place to be, a purpose and a time frame, rather than just random journeys to various parts of the world.

Finally, a volunteer break can be really good for your work prospects and career development. Potential employers are often impressed by a stint of helping out a charity organisation while you're travelling as it shows lots of values they appreciate, such as commitment, determination, generosity and patience. And don't forget you can use your volunteer time to progress your chosen career path quicker; for example if you want to be an engineer, you can find a placement using engineer's skills, or if you're into marine biology, coral and fish monitoring in the Caribbean ticks all the right boxes.

IS IT RIGHT FOR YOU?

The first factor to take into consideration is how long you've got; will this be a year or more, or a short stint of volunteering as part of your travel experience?

The next thing to consider is how much you have to spend. Don't be fooled into thinking that because you'll be volunteering, it won't cost you. Some people are really surprised to discover that volunteering costs money, even though they're giving their time and labour for free, but the reality is that the majority of volunteer organisations have to charge you for the experience, from a few hundred pounds to thousands. Because you'll only be out in the field for a short time, probably a year or less, your money is needed to cover the costs of hosting and supporting volunteers with things like healthcare and food, plus accommodation and training.

You have to be prepared to live at a very basic level, some-times without hot water and electricity, so if you love your home comforts and think you'd have a miserable time without them, you have to be realistic and possibly avoid developing countries.

Being able to accept other cultures, however different they are from your own, is also crucial to enjoying the volunteer experience. There may be some magical aspects of lifestyles that you encounter, but there are also likely to be traditions that you don't agree with and it's not your job to march into a community and inflict Western change on all levels.

I've mentioned that volunteering can be wonderful for your self-esteem and confidence, however, this shouldn't be your only reason for doing it. If you're running away from something, such as a broken relationship, you're not going to be instantly happier on your placement. In fact, being alone in a foreign country initially with no friends or even someone to talk to in the same language can be incredibly isolating, so do make sure you're going for the right reasons.

You might want to make your volunteer experience relevant to work or study that you currently do, such as if you're a doctor you could take a medical caring option, or a journalist could help set up a newspaper. However, don't for a minute be put off the idea of volunteering because you think you have to have a skill. Pretty much anyone can volunteer (subject to police checks if you're working with kids) and often it's your time and energy that's invaluable rather than a specific skill, plus it can be immensely satisfying to learn something new while you're there.

Timing is also crucial for some volunteering; for example if you want to work in a school while you're away, you're going to need to coincide your travel with term times.

As well as volunteering, do you want to do any other activities while you're there? Some organisations offer the chance to learn new skills or take trips while you're being a volunteer.

You also need to decide whether you want to volunteer for a charity or set up something yourself, such as contacting a school or hospital in a developing country directly and asking if they need assistance. Most people opt for the charity route, because it means there's already an organised structure in place; you know that your help is genuinely needed and will have an effect; and the money you pay is usually to cover costs and the rest goes to the charity's causes, so you know your cash is going to the right pockets.

WHAT ARE THE OPTIONS?

It's easy to decide you want to do some volunteer work while you're away, what's not so easy is picking the right project for you from the thousands on offer around the world. You may have a cause you feel passionately about already, such as animal conservation or HIV, which narrows down your search, but many people just want to lend a hand. To help you, I've split up the volunteering sector into two easy groups: community-based action project, covering everything from teaching to healthcare; and conservation, encompassing all work with animals and nature.

Community-based

If you're a people person, social and outgoing, this type of placement is going to appeal. It's a broad section encompassing a wide range of amazing placements which are primarily people-focused; think helping to build a well, teaching in a school, assisting in hospitals, social work, orphanages, schools and sports centres. Often, you don't need any qualifications (unless otherwise specifically stated), just the ability to be able to provide care and empathy.

This type of placement can be incredibly rewarding, but if you're the sort of person that finds it hard to leave troubles behind you at the end of a working day, it might be a good idea to combine several placements. This will give you the flexibility to travel around and ensure you don't get too emotionally attached to one specific cause or place.

Conservation-based

If you're an environmentalist, a nature lover or just want to hang out in a beautiful location for a while, conservation-based volunteer work could be the way forward for you.

There are opportunities around the world to work with some of the planet's most magnificent animals, such as lions, wild dogs, leopards, elephants, cheetahs or orphaned orangutans. However, it can be equally as rewarding to work on less glamorous placements, from iguana tagging to penguin monitoring. If you're keen on marine life, then placements to work alongside sharks, whales, fish and dolphins could be for you. Or how about coral and reef exploration and protection?

WHERE TO GO?

There are so many volunteer placements available around the world it can be hard to pinpoint where you want to be, which is why it can be a help to choose the type of volunteering you want to do first, and make this fit to the country.

Alternatively, you may want to choose the country or location and then hunt around for an exciting project while you're there. If you're opting to do it this way, make sure you do your research and find out whether it's going to be a country that you will feel happy to live and work in for a prolonged period of time. Guidebooks are a good starting point; learn about local customs, beliefs, history, food, climate and geography of the place.

Top Travel Tip

Call the tourist board of a country you're keen to visit and request information on volunteer programmes.

Also try to seek out past volunteers from countries you're interested in online to ask them for the low down. It's impossible to cover all of the incredible programmes available, but here's a brief round-up to give you an idea of what's on offer around the globe.

USA & Canada

North America is a popular choice and it's particularly good if you don't want to live in a developing country while volunteering. If the thought of the extremes of the East, from weather to language barriers, is off-putting to you then a stint in the States could be the perfect introduction to volunteer travel. Some of the most popular programmes on offer include summer camps, perfect to fill up university holidays. There are also lots of environmental placements to take up, such as seal observation in Alaska, helping to protect the mountainous and geologically diverse Nevada landscape and even monitoring wildlife and nature in New York City.

Central America

The jewel in Central America's volunteering crown is Costa Rica, which boasts some of the greatest biodiversity on the planet. One of the most popular pursuits is the protection of sea turtles along with helping to restore and protect forests. But it's not just about the nature, there are lots of people projects too from women's cooperatives to helping to renovate buildings. Also consider less well-known opportunities, but just as important, such as coral monitoring in Belize, aiding families and orphans in Guatemala, implementing clean water and sanitation in Honduras and helping to build homes and digging wells in the Dominican Republic, where one-fifth of the country lives below the poverty line.

South America

The obvious choice here is rainforest conservation. The Amazon jungle crosses Brazil, Peru, Ecuador, Colombia, Guyana and Venezuela, and with deforestation the size of France, it's never been more important to help protect the forests through patrols and assessing biodiversity, from sloths to tree frogs. If that's not your bag, then the oceans around South America are teaming with marine life which scientists are continually monitoring, like manatees and hammerhead sharks. The environment is now big business here, so helping out in eco lodges is a fun and sociable option, or lending a hand on an organic farm. You can also get involved with sustainable community projects, such as house building and sanitation. Or if you want some city action, how about working with street kids in city slums such as Rio de Janeiro?

Europe

The rich countries of Europe don't seem the obvious starting point when it comes to volunteer work. It might not seem as worthy and your Facebook pictures may not look as extreme – a shot of you digging a well in Africa in 45-degree heat certainly says cool and interesting gap year – but Europe can be a great option if you want to stay in your comfort zone, can't go away for a long period of time and don't want to travel too far. Programmes are as diverse as studying bottlenose dolphins off the coast of Croatia to seed-planting in a Spanish desert.

Africa

It's a Mecca for volunteering and little wonder; it boasts some of one the most incredible experiences and landscapes on earth. Colourful, vibrant, wild, cultural, sometimes dangerous and with heartbreaking poverty in places, you're in for a rollercoaster ride of excitement with a placement here. Kenya and South Africa are very popular for wildlife conservation work, such as trail and camp maintenance, animal census and helping with research for endangered animals, such as Angolan black monkeys or the white rhino. There is an HIV/AIDS epidemic in parts of Africa, and the consequences of this means that there are lots of volunteer programmes geared to this. Botswana, Kenya, Tanzania, Malawi and Zambia have all been hard hit by the virus, and volunteer programmes range from working in orphanages to assisting in medical clinics.

Asia

It's the largest continent in the world, so you're bound to find something here that appeals. Cambodia and Laos are currently the hot places to make your mark. Teaching English is in real demand in both countries, and with literacy below 70 per cent, it's a worthwhile cause. In India, around 250 million people, 25 per cent of the population, live below the poverty line, so community development programmes, such as working with street children or helping the elderly are in abundance. The stunning Indian Ocean island of Sri Lanka may be more associated with honeymoons, but it was devastated in the Tsunami in 2004 and relief work is still needed to help resort villages. In Thailand, marine and coastal research centres are a major source of conservation programmes.

Australia & Pacific

As you'd expect, wildlife and marine conservation is the big story in Oz, from tree planting to monitoring the critically endangered hawksbill turtles on the Great Barrier Reef. The paradise islands of the Pacific are possibly the most idyllic places on the planet for a volunteer placement. However, the projects are a million miles away from beach holidays in five-star resorts. In the Cook Islands, for example, places in demand include assisting with healthcare, painting and repairing buildings, and teaching English.

VOLUNTEER ORGANISATIONS

Whether or not to pay to participate in a volunteering project is a choice that you need to make. By working as a self-funded volunteer who covers their own costs, you're ensuring the often economically poor communities that you'll be working with are not having to subsidise you in any way. You should view your financial contribution as your required donation to the project.

However, one of the biggest concerns of most volunteers is that they don't know how much of the money they're handing over goes towards helping communities or conservation.

Top Travel Tip

Ask volunteer companies for a breakdown of how their money's spent; such as 30 per cent donation to cause, 30 per cent spent on providing food and accommodation for volunteers, 30 per cent on running costs and 10 per cent profit. This way you can be sure your money is going to a good cause and not into the pockets of rich tour operators.

Naturally it helps to go with a well-established, well-known organisation, such as the Voluntary Service Overseas (VSO, www.VSO.org.uk), which is an independent, international development charity whose main aim is to fight poverty in developing countries, from building houses to HIV care. Placements range from one month to two years and cover 33 countries, and people of all ages, from 18 to 75, take part.

If you're a student, then there are more than 500 projects to take a look at on the http://statravel.i-to-i.com website, from environmental projects in Borneo to wildlife placements in Africa. It also offers add-ons, such as climbing Mount Kilimanjaro while you're volunteering in Tanzania.

Environmentalists will want to take a look at Earthwatch, www.earthwatch.org, a charity founded in 1971 which encourages people worldwide to be involved in scientific research all over the world, plus education to promote understanding and sustaining the environment. On a smaller scale Biosphere Expeditions, www.biosphere-expeditions.org, offers wildlife and environmental opportunities to work alongside scientists. I joined their expedition to track leopards in Oman, to establish whether there were still big cats in the Musandam Peninsula and found it a very rewarding experience – best of all it's a non-profit organisation.

If you want to volunteer in the United States or Canada, for things such as summer camp, have a look on www.bunac. org.uk, or if you want to browse through lots of volunteer organisations, log on to www.do-it.org.uk and go into the Volunteering overseas section. Here you'll find lots of websites and a brief description of what they are offering, such as Blue Ventures, marine conservation in Madagascar.

FUNDRAISING

If you have your heart set on volunteering abroad but can't afford to go, then it's worth considering raising money to fund your trip. Not only does fundraising give you a goal and make the placement seem even more worthwhile, remember that by organising fundraising events, you also raise awareness of issues in the country you're travelling to.

Fundraising has to be planned well in advance and you'll need to draw up sponsorship forms and a letter of endorsement from the company or charity that you're travelling with. You need to let people know that the organisation isn't in a position to cover your costs, so by helping you people are directly helping the charity too.

What to do

Fundraising might remind you of the sort of thing you used to do when you were little, such as selling cakes to raise money for a church roof in the Brownies. The fact is that fundraising when you're old isn't that different.

The more unique your event the better. Use your imagination, and organise something that will suit your personality and the resources you can call upon. Some of the most popular forms of fundraising include a raffle (ask local shops to donate an item); a cultural event, such as a music or comedy night; a sponsored run, swim or cycle; and a car boot sale (beg family and friends to donate any unwanted items to you). Some volunteers also approach local businesses to ask for donations. Approach your local paper and try to get a story written about your intentions, and include a phone number so any sympathetic readers can get in touch and help out or pledge money.

Top Travel Tip

The most important element to successful fundraising is determination. Remember, you are collecting for a worthwhile cause, so don't be ashamed to ask people for donations.

Raising awareness

When organising a fundraising event, try to get as much publicity for it as possible. Local and college newspapers and radio stations will often give such events a mention; use noticeboards in the locality; and most importantly make sure everyone you know spreads the word. If you are using a venue for the event, try to use your contacts to find somewhere free of charge. For ticketed events, print out plenty of tickets – people may buy them even if they cannot attend.

Targets

It is important that you and your sponsors know how much money you aim to raise and what it will be spent on such as flights, accommodation, food and charity donation.

Checklist

* Choose whether you're suited to
  community or conservation programmes ☑
* Do you want to pay to volunteer? ☑
* Decide on your destination(s) ☑
* Look at volunteer organisations' programmes ☑
* Find out how your money contribution would
  be spent in the organisation ☑
* Consider fundraising to raise money for
  your trip ☑

Chapter 6
Backpacking

Backpacking has become synonymous with students in their gap year, but the reality is that there are thousands of different types of backpackers from 18 to 80 heading off each year to enjoy this cheap and cheerful form of travel.

If you're not quite sure what the term means, there are three things that define backpackers; budget travel, independence and flexibility. The key to this form of seeing the world is that it's not all about fancy hotels and resorts, it's more about authentic (and cheap) places to stay which you can arrive at unexpectedly and leave at a moment's notice. The fact that your trip isn't arranged through tour operators or any organisation means that you're not beholden to anyone, and can basically go where you want (within reason and money permitting) while you're away.

Backpacking allows you the fun of hearing about a great place to visit, and then heading off into the unknown to find it. In addition, backpackers usually use public transport while away, because it's low cost and more authentic, plus travel as light as possible, with just essentials and some extra clothing in their rucksack.

FAMOUS BACKPACKER TRAILS

There are well-worn backpacker trails all over the globe, and there are always hundreds of people passing through the tried and tested routes, so it's very easy to make friends and have a constant source of people to hang out with. Here are a few of the best-loved trails of the last 50 years.

1960s

It's hard to pinpoint exactly when backpacking became popular, but it can certainly be traced back to the hippy trails of the 1960s. These trails were the journeys taken by European hippies from Europe overland through to Asia. The aim was to get there as cheaply as possible, so much of the transport was through hitchhiking or cheap buses. A typical route for thousands of hippies was from London or Amsterdam through Istanbul, Teheran, Herat, Kabul, Peshawar and Lahore to final ports of call Goa or Kathmandu.

1970s

As well as the trail above, another popular route in the 70s was through Eastern Europe taking in Turkey, via Syria, Jordan, Iraq and Iran, then east to southern India, Sri Lanka and even Australia.

1980s

Conflicts between the Soviet Union and Afghanistan made the Eastern Europe route increasingly inaccessible in the 80s, so alternative trails evolved, such as the north Africa trail, including Tunisia, Morocco and Sinai.

1990s

As political and military conflicts made the original trails unworkable, backpackers started travelling west to South America for inspiration, nicknamed the Gringo Trail by locals. It's not a set trail, but many seem to travel around Peru, Ecuador, Chile and Bolivia, including at least all or some of the following: Lima, the Andes, Amazon, Nazca Lines, Cusco, Inca trail, Lake Titicaca and La Paz.

2000s

The modern-day equivalent of the 60s hippy trail is the Banana Pancake trail, which is a well-trodden route through Southeast Asia and so called because of the legions of cheap cafés and restaurants that have sprung up to serve up sweet breakfasts to broke and hungry Western backpackers. There's no one route, but Bangkok, Koh Phi Phi and Koh Samui in Thailand, Varanasi in India, Vang Vieng in Laos, Melaka in Malaysia, Bali in Indonesia and Borneo are firm favourites.

DRUGS

As you'd expect from a form of travel inspired by the hippy generation, there are often drugs available at many of the key backpacking stop-offs. It's a reality you need to be aware of as drug use and possession can be a much more serious situation overseas than in the UK.

Even if you've never indulged in Britain before, it can be extremely tempting to have a try while you're feeling independent, confident and letting your hair down in a country far away from the pressures of home. However, it's really important that you think twice before recklessly taking anything while you're away, from cannabis to Ecstasy, for several reasons.

The first is that although you may find there are a lot of drugs available on the street and that you're approached frequently, probably more than at home, that doesn't mean that the laws are more lenient. In fact it's usually the opposite case, with many countries, particularly in the east, handing out very harsh penalties if you're found in possession. Turkey, Thailand, Singapore, Indonesia, Iran, Algeria and Malaysia can and have actually imposed the death penalty for drugs-related offences.

Other destinations will hand out a very long sentence in prison, which are often much tougher and have far poorer conditions than a UK prison.

Something you may not be aware of is that some drug dealers in countries such as Thailand actually have agreements with the local police force to inform them of tourist clients in exchange for them keeping their patch without hassle. You therefore face the risk of imprisonment or having to pay out a massive bribe (probably most of your trip money) to the police, every time you buy some drugs. Basically, the message I'm trying to get across is that by accepting drugs, you're risking your life in some countries and your freedom in many more.

Top Travel Tip

Don't put yourself under needless scrutiny of the authorities for any medical drugs you may be carrying around. With any medication, make sure you have a proper and appropriate prescription, which should put a stop to any interviews and long delays at airports.

WHAT TO TAKE

I've covered packing in Chapter 2, but backpacking is a bit more specific. You're going to be travelling for a long period of time, staying in basic accommodation without many home comforts, such as a washing machine, and may sometimes not be able to have a bed for the night. You're also going to be travelling on public transport a lot of the time, so you don't want to be weighed down with bulky bags, which take up vital room. With this in mind, packing needs to be as tight, light and as useful as possible.

For your checklist, I'd suggest:

Clothing

3 T-shirts — they're light and easy to roll up.
2 long sleeved tops — it's essential to cover up sometimes, such as in mosquito ridden areas or in strict Muslim countries.
1 pair of trousers — cargo trousers with loads of pockets are really useful.
1 pair of jeans — they're hardwearing and are accepted pretty much anywhere.
1 sarong — men and women can wear this extremely adaptable piece of clothing which can be wrapped around the hips for a skirt or tied at the neck to make a dress.
1 long skirt.
1 sun dress/light trousers.
1 swimming trunks/costume/bikini.
1 head scarf/pashmina — this is really useful for covering the head and shoulders in a Muslim country or to enter places of worship, and can also help keep you warm when temperatures drop.
1 pair of shorts — bear in mind they aren't acceptable attire in some countries.
7 sets of underwear.
4 pairs of socks.
1 pair of walking boots — though as these are very heavy only take them if you know they're going to be needed. If you're going to be in a beach location for three months, don't bother.
1 hat — particularly if you're travelling to a hot country.
1 pair of flip-flops or sandals.
1 pair of comfortable trainers.

Essential items

1 sleeping bag — vital if you're ever sleeping outdoors and
   you may want to use it in some hostels if they're not
   very clean.
1 water bottle — really important in hotter, third world
   countries where drinking water may be contaminated.
1 Swiss Army knife.
1 toiletries bag — with pared down make-up and wash
   stuff, like combined shampoo and conditioner; don't
   forget your toothbrush!
1 first-aid kit.
1 pair of sunglasses — not just for posing, but essential in
   very hot countries where direct sun can damage your
   eyes.
1 towel.
1 mess kit — knife, fork, spoon and plastic bowl and cup.

Non-essential items (but it's good to have them!)

1 camera.
1 mobile phone — useful for keeping in touch with home,
   as an alarm clock and calculator.
1 money belt.
1 pack of cards — you'll find it's a great way to make
   friends and kills time on long journeys.
1 small, light bag for day use.
1 money belt.
1 MP3 player.
1 battery charger for electrical items.

1 pen — always useful for form filling, writing down addresses and directions and getting email contacts as you travel.

Top Travel Tip

Take a roll of bin bags – You can keep dirty clothes in them, put your backpack in one if you want to keep it waterproof and even wear one yourself to protect you from the elements!

What to leave behind

Your hairdryer
Yes, most girls stress about bad hair days, but it's not an issue when you're travelling, as everyone else is in the same boat (sometimes literally). Even if you're thinking of buying a small fold-up travel one, it's taking up vital space in your backpack plus it's unlikely you're regularly going to have somewhere to plug it in as many hostels don't have sockets in the rooms. Instead, take a handful of hair ties, wear a hat or let your hair dry naturally; it's actually very liberating to ditch the beauty products and can look great.

Valuables
Don't take anything that's irreplaceable, such as the diamond bracelet and earrings your granny left you. Backpackers are sometimes victims of theft, plus there's the risk of lost luggage when you fly or take transfers, so it's not worth taking things that are very precious to you.

Food

You may be worried that the place you're going to won't have your favourite fizzy drink brand or tea bags, and the chances are it won't! But that's a good thing. You're travelling to a new country, so embrace the new dishes and drinks you're about to try, that's part of the whole fun of travel. Besides, you can actually get hold of a lot of your favourite products in super-markets around the world anyway.

Checklist

* Plan a basic route ☑
* Take necessary precautions from drug risks ☑
* Buy/collect together your essential items ☑
* Decide what to leave behind ☑

Chapter 7
Flashpacking

This is a term to define a new generation of traveller who may look visibly similar to their backpacking brethren (scruffy clothes and unwashed hair) but differ in one very important element – they've got cash.

I've searched high and low for the definitive description of a flashpacker: backpacking on a bigger budget; backpacking with better gadgets; older backpackers with a disposable income. Really, this new travel movement is a combination of all of the above, plus, and this is key, a love of insider travel knowledge. It's about people that want to mix a bit of slumming it with a little bit of luxury too. It can also encompass those that are time short but cash rich – they don't have a year to waste and so choose to travel quicker and more efficiently; for instance, rather than taking a week to overland it across Thailand on a bus, they'll jump on a cheap internal flight.

However, what does unite backpackers and flashpackers is an aversion to tour operators and fixed itineraries, the quest for far-flung exciting destinations and situations, and often the need to get away for a longer period of time than your average holiday.

ARE YOU A FLASHPACKER?

You need to discover if you're a flashpacker before you set off as it's a different way of travelling, with a different set of problems and solutions. A good place to start is whether you love your home comforts. If you think the *idea* of backpacking is brilliant, but secretly know that you couldn't do without your MP3 player, hairdryer, mobile phone and laptop for a minute, then you're definitely in flashpacker territory. A typical flashpacker may be on a career break. But, of course, you could just be on your two-week summer holiday – but rather than join the hordes on the beach, it's a romp across the rainforest for you.

If you already work and have a disposable income, you're likely to be in flashpacker camp. Ditto if you've been backpacking in your youth and now you're a bit older feel that you desperately want to regain that sense of freedom, but would rather not sleep in cockroach-infested dormitories again.

The term may also apply to you if are thinking about being budget conscious with accommodation, but want to blow a bit of cash on amazing experiences, like bungee jumping and swimming with dolphins. And the term is certainly you if you fancy unique boutique hotel-type retreats, which are very much local and often cheap, but certainly not a youth hostel.

WHERE TO GO?

Flashpacking certainly includes some similar places to traditional backpacking routes as discussed in the last chapter; think Morocco, Thailand and India. However, flashpackers often seem drawn to the more expensive or hard-to-get-to-destinations, which may be out of reach for some backpackers.

Fiji, for example, is actually quite pricey, but the sort of idyllic, far-flung exotic place that a flashpacker will rush to find. Bhutan is proving immensely hip, what with the complicated visa system, limited entry numbers and lack of tourists. Ditto China, which is prime flashpacker territory now that it's slowly opening up to tourism, and Indonesia is always a winner, particularly the smaller islands.

Flashpackers really like to get into the culture of a country, so are more likely to prefer a small village somewhere with no, or few, tourists, than a well-worn trail where you're as likely to meet Dave from Deptford on his gap year than you are a genuine local.

Still after a bargain, they're likely to head to a sought-after destination out of season, when prices are halved and you're less likely to meet hordes of holiday makers.

WHERE TO STAY?

Accommodation is one of the key areas where flashpackers differ from backpackers. Though neither wants to spend a fortune, they part company when it comes to quality and amenities. Consequently, hostels and budget hotels have had to step up to the mark and cater for this new breed of more demanding traveller.

Flashpackers aren't content with a fusty old mattress and no amenities, they're willing to shell out a bit more for some home comforts and better décor. Yes, they, like backpackers, don't spend much time in their room so don't want to pay high prices, but they demand a certain quality.

Pod hotels

Step forward some hostels offering more up-market accommodation – think Internet cafes, tasteful furniture, Wi-Fi and power showers (for more information on hostels and home-stays, refer to Chapter 2). A hostel isn't the flashpacker's only accommodation of choice however; they're also interested in innovative new places, such as the rise in pod hotels around the world – ultra cheap places to stay with a room the size of a postage stamp but all mod cons and inspired by Japan's capsule hotels.

Some hostels and budget hotels have realised a need to evolve in order to meet the changing demands of travellers, with the emergence of pod hotels in Japan, London and New York, where the incredibly cheap (and tiny) rooms come with flat screen TV, Wi-Fi and funky furnishings. The Pod Hotel (www.podhotel.com) in Manhattan is targeting the stylish but thrifty traveller, and the cramped rooms (some single, some double and some with bunks) have an iPod docking station, LCD TVs, dimmer lights, rain head showers and bright fashionable furnishings, and are about the cheapest rooms you'll get in NY.

Yotel (www.yotel.com) in London and Amsterdam is a great example of this new trend, with cabin bedrooms, which come with all the posh hotel trimmings, like fluffy towels and heated mirrors, but in a tiny space. Qbic Hotels (qbichotels.com); EasyJet Hotels (easyhotel.com); Cube Hotels (www.cube-hotels.com), which offer pods in the mountains of Austria and Switzerland; Tune Hotels (www.tunehotels.com) in Malaysia and Borneo; and Capsule Hotels in Japan, such as www.capsuleinn.com, are all offering similar low budget, more style options.

Chic retreats

Fashionable, sometimes rustic, but always boutique and local; this is the ideal sort of accommodation for a flashpacker who wants to shell out for more than a hostel.

It's all about places that hardly anyone else knows about; tiny six-room retreats with no air conditioning, just open windows and dining on fresh, local food. Along with word of mouth, the Internet is the best friend of the flashpacker, as it's where they can discover the cheapest, chicest places to stay.

Among the favourite sites is www.i-escape.com, which offers all kinds of idyllic options, from beach huts in Sri Lanka to a rustic finca in the Canary Islands. Travel Intelligence, www.travelintelligence.com, is a really good site where travel writers review boutique hotels that you're unlikely to find on many tour operator's books.

Chic Retreats, www.chicretreats.com, is pricey but offers tiny, beautifully designed places to stay around the globe with 30 rooms or less. Hip Hotels, www.hiphotels.com is a similar high-end place to seek out great places to stay, as is Mr&Mrs Smith, www.mrandmrssmith.com. Tablet Hotels, www.tablet hotels.com, which markets itself at global nomads (ie flashpackers!) is leading the way in offering hip, local getaways, often offering suggestions of hideaways a couple of hours from a city centre as well as the coolest places in town. It even has Tablet Tunes available to download to your laptop or MP3, which are country or hotel-specific, perfect for the gadget- and music-loving traveller. Epoque Hotels, www.epoque hotels. com, also specialises in boutique retreats worldwide, with a good 'specials' section offering promotions and money off.

In Europe, Alastair Sawday's recommendations are numerous and include some real gems, www.sawdays.co.uk.

Top Travel Tip

For intimate, stylish and reasonable priced riads in Morocco, log on to www.hipmarrakech.com.

WHAT TO TAKE

A flashbacker's gear differs from a backpacker's, mainly because it's much more high tech.

Essential items

As well as the usual socks, underwear, jeans, t-shirts and sarongs listed in the previous chapter, essentials for a flash-packer usually include:

* BlackBerry.
* Digital camera and download cable — for sending photos back home.
* MP3 player — with the latest travel guides downloaded onto it.
* Memory stick.
* Laptop.
* Credit card.
* Luggage padlock.

Non-essentials

* Pocket warmer.
* GPS system.
* Blow-up travel pillow.

What not to take

* Guidebooks — every savvy flashpacker has Internet access or guides stored on their MP3 players so their info is always bang up to date.

WORD OF WARNING

If you're a flashpacker or about to become one, the same rules about looking after yourself, and your belongings, while you're away apply.

If you've got a lot of gizmos, make sure you have insurance to cover them all – you'd be surprised at how many policies don't cover extras like laptops.

Make sure you continually back up your photos, videos and notes. It would be heartbreaking to transfer pictures to your laptop and erase the camera memory card, only to have your computer stolen. That's why it's a good idea to take a small memory stick.

Top Travel Tip

Try to buy as much as possible on your credit card, as this is insured should you come across any fraud. Unfortunately, not all debit cards allow money to be claimed back if the card is stolen or the details used.

FOOD

With regards to food, www.flashpackguideinfo says that the difference between flashpackers and backpackers is the former are likely to put on weight during a trip and the latter to lose it! Trying a country's cuisine, whether it's a street stall or hip restaurant, is all part of the travel experience and not something just to provide enough energy to get through the next full moon party.

Checklist

* Are you a flashpacker? ☑
* Decide on your destination ☑
* How long do you want to travel for? ☑
* Where to stay; consult Internet sites ☑
* Buy/find essential packing items ☑
* Gadget check ☑
* Back up photos/videos/notes ☑
* Make sure you have travel insurance for your gizmos ☑

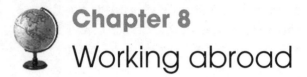

Chapter 8
Working abroad

If you really want to get away and see the world but know that you don't have the finances, one option could be to earn as you go. Working while you're at a destination, from bar work to teaching English, also brings you other benefits asides from a wage. It's a fantastic way of making friends while you're overseas plus you often gain a completely different cultural perspective – rather than just being another tourist you become part of a community.

WHAT SORT OF JOB?

There are lots of job opportunities overseas, but not all of them are particularly well paid or skilled. The first thing that you need to decide is whether you want a job to provide a bit of extra spending money in your pocket, or whether this is going to fund your whole trip. You'll also need to think about whether you want your work to be career and CV-enhancing, and how long and in what conditions you're prepared to work, as this will seriously affect your job choice.

Childcare

There are lots of nanny or au pair job opportunities overseas, so if you love kids but don't want to teach, this could be a great option for you. You could take on a private placement for a specific family. The bonus of this is that you're likely to be able to live-in and so get free board and a room, but this of course also means that you're more likely to be on the job most of the time. Another option is to join a large tour operator, such as Thompson (www.thompson.co.uk/jobs), which always needs crèche reps on board. However you search for the job, you'll need to be organised and arrange your placement in advance, as it's unlikely that simply showing up in a country and trying to find childcare work will bring much success. For a job in a family, have a look at www.nannyjob.co.uk, which has work placements in the UK and abroad.

Top Travel Tip

Take a look at Gap Year, www.gapyear.com/care-work, which has lots of jobs advertised for au pairs.

Fruit picking

This is the ideal sort of job if you just want to earn some extra cash while you're away rather than feeling tied to one place through contract work. Although the pay is low, it's a popular option as it's outdoors, often in the sunshine and great if you're with a friend or want to meet fellow travellers. Australia has lots of fruit-picking jobs, with most on offer in the summer months (December to May). You'll be filling buckets full of fruit and are paid at the end of the day per bucket; it's unusual to be paid by the hour. The downside of the job is that it's physically demanding and the farms are often in remote areas. It's important to check that there is a hostel in the area where pickers can stay, or whether the farm provides accommodation, although this isn't the norm. For picking jobs around the world, take a look at www.pickingjobs.com.

Kibbutzim

A kibbutz, found in Israel, is a form of communal living traditionally based on agriculture but can also include things like factories too. All property is communally owned, any income is shared within the kibbutz and everyone dines together. You could find yourself doing anything from cleaning the loos and milking cows, to working on an orange grove and preparing fish. There are currently 256 kibbutzim in Israel made up of around 106,000 people, so there's lots of potential to find work and meet people from all over the world. Apart from a flight to Israel, the only other thing you'll need to shell out for is a small administration and insurance fee to the Kibbutz Volunteers Office in Tel Aviv, where you'll need to register before going to your kibbutz. For more information, log on to www.kibbutz.org.il/eng/.

Ski season

If you want to earn for some of the year and then travel for the rest, then seasonal work is a great option to consider. In the winter months in Europe, Canada and the US, the ski season is an obvious option if you're a snow lover.

Ski repping, catering work, cleaning and childcare are all options in ski resorts, as well as ski and snowboard instructors if you're qualified. Working with a winter tour operator, like Mark Warner, is a great idea if you want to get your board and food paid for, but these jobs are in demand so it's a good idea to plan ahead and get in early, particularly as the language barrier and legal difficulties can make finding work on the spot in European resorts very difficult.

If you're thinking of being a chalet rep, you'll need to be prepared to organise things like daily menus, and also be prepared to muck in and help change laundry and clean the loos; it's not all fun on the slopes! Local bar, shop or restaurant work is also an option in some of the bigger resorts, and the pay can actually be better than chalet work, although an ability to speak languages may be more important for this role. However, working a ski season is immense fun and you do of course get time off to hone your own ski or board skills.

Top Travel Tip

Check out www.natives.co.uk, which has an A to Z of jobs in the ski industry.

The best time to start applying for winter snow jobs in hotels, chalets and bars is from May onwards; to get you started take a look at www.hotrecruit.co.uk, www.anyworkanywhere.com, www.natives.co.uk. Popular resorts with Brits include Les Arcs, Chamonix and Mirabelle in France, Mayrhofen in Austria and Verbier in Switzerland, but it's best to have lots of options, as you don't know if you'll secure a place in your favourite resort.

Summer camps

The USA and Canada are the top places for summer camp work and are extremely popular with young Brits. The lack of a language barrier is an immediate plus, working with kids is a fun option and accommodation and food is provided. BUNAC (The British Universities North America Club), www.bunac.org.uk, is a non-profit organisation, which for the last 45 years has helped arrange working holidays.

Summer Camp USA is one of the most well-known schemes, and offers 19- to 35-year-olds the chance to spend eight or nine weeks between May and August teaching kids activities. You don't need specific qualifications, but you're likely to be given a placement to suit your skills and supervise children from 6 to 16.

If being directly in contact with kids all day isn't your idea of heaven, then you may also be interested in KAMP USA (Kitchens and Maintenance Programme) which offers jobs behind the scenes in summer camps, such as working in a kitchen, dining room, office or helping with general odd jobs. Have a look at www.bunac.org/uk/kampusa for more information.

Teaching English

One of the most popular job choices for Brits is to teach English overseas. Not only is it a relatively well-paid form of work, it's also a fantastic way to get involved in a community and provides a good social network from the moment you land.

In order to get a proper placement, you need to invest in a TEFL (Teach English as a Foreign Language) course and get a certificate. There are courses all over the country, and they are usually four weeks although there are also long weekend intensive courses, introductory placements and home-study options.

The vast range of countries where TEFL teachers are required includes:

Spain, Germany, France, Italy, Greece, Austria, Russia, Turkey, Slovak Republic, Croatia, Serbia, Lithuania, Poland, Czech Republic, Taiwan, South Korea, China, Japan, Indonesia, Thailand, Vietnam, Peru, Ecuador, Columbia, Brazil, Chile, Argentina, USA, England, Mexico, Bahrain, Qatar, Tanzania and Zambia. Basically, the world's your oyster!

The plus side of teaching English is that you get a fixed contract, anything from three months to two years; often have accommodation supplied by your employer; earn a steady income which can fund your trip and onward sightseeing adventures; total immersion in another culture; and you get to meet likeminded teachers on your course and probably in your place of employment. It also looks good on your CV.

The downside of TEFL is that if you're on a contract, you can't just take off on a whim if you get itchy feet. The hours you work will depend on the type of placement you have, and can vary from a few hours a day to a full working week; check this before you sign if you don't want to be 9 to 5. I have heard complaints before that some wage offers aren't as high as teachers would like, however, if you don't have any money to start off with, it's a great start!

Top Travel Tip

If you're interested in TEFL, then there are lots of websites providing information on courses, including www.tefltraining.co.uk, www.tefl.co.uk, www.cactustefl.com, www.onlinetefl.com, and www.oxfordtefl.com.

If you're interested in teaching English in the East, particularly Japan, then also have a look at JET Programme (Japanese Exchange & Teaching), www.jetprogramme.org. Each year the JET Programme, with the aid of the Japanese Ministry of Foreign Affairs, recruits thousands of new participants to come to Japan. These recruits are assigned to be either Assistant Language Teachers (ALTs) who provide language instruction in elementary, junior and senior high schools; Coordinators for International Relations (CIRs) who work in communities on international exchange activities; or Sports Exchange Advisors (SEAs) who promote international exchange through sports. Participants are placed with local government organisations throughout Japan, including large cities, small and medium-sized towns, and rural farming and fishing villages.

Top Travel Tip

For ideas all around the world, take a look at www.seasonworkers.com, you can even apply for jobs online if something catches your eye.

RED TAPE

You do really need to make certain that your travel documents and entry permits allow you to undertake work legally in your chosen destination and that you're not in violation of any visas, work permits or other agreements that would make it difficult to enter a particular country.

Some travellers work illegally, picking up the odd job here and there to pay their way, but if you're looking at earning more than the odd bar shift, you need to get your paperwork in order. We're all used to the idea of working freely within the EU since the single market came into play, but that doesn't mean the rest of the world is now open for you to work and play where you like.

Before you take the plunge a key thing to find out is: what is the economy like of the country you want to work in? The laws of the country are often designed to protect the country's economy and workforce. Political considerations may also mean that visas are easier/more difficult to obtain; beyond the EU, Commonwealth countries may be more receptive to British nationals looking to work or travel.

You must find out what type of visa you need. For example, do you need work-travel visas for tourism, which are far easier to get for casual jobs than those needed for a graduate-type position.

Top Travel Tip

If you have skills, try and match them to a country. Some countries have shortages in some areas, such as nurses or English teachers; check out government sites for published lists of shortage areas.

Try to get a written offer of work. If you've secured an offer of work from an employer who feels you are essential to them, they are likely to be more persuasive of the authorities than a speculative applicant. Work out how long you're going to want to stay in a country – shorter visas and work permits are easier to obtain than longer ones.

BUNAC is a real help when is comes to work authorisation in the USA, Canada, Australia and New Zealand. For Canada you can obtain an Open Work Authorisation Visa (only available through BUNAC).

Checklist

* Find out what sort of job is right for you   ☑
* Match your skills to the job   ☑
* Or, find a job to improve your skills   ☑
* Use the Internet to explore your options   ☑
* Find out what red tape is involved in work overseas   ☑

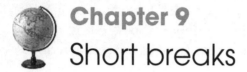

Chapter 9
Short breaks

Gap years, 12 months' backpacking and volunteering for six months are all well and good, but what if you just don't have that much time to spare? This chapter shows you just how much you can get out of a month away and still feel like you've had the trip of a lifetime.

Round the World (RTW) travel was previously associated with year-out budget travel and backpacking. In the new millennium however, RTW has taken on a more up-market, short-duration, package-driven form.

The significant growth within the Short Break market has been driven by the consumer's increasingly hectic lifestyle, increasing the desire for short holidays. Rising levels of consumer expenditure have also bolstered the market, together with the proliferation of low-cost air routes appealing to the more adventurous consumer's desire to experience new destinations.

WHERE ON EARTH?

It's easy to think that just because you've only got a few weeks holiday a year you won't have time to have a real backpacker-esque experience – you'd be amazed at how much you can cram into just a few weeks.

What you have to be is organised and slightly ruthless, ditching some places in favour of others, as there simply won't be time to pack everything in.

First off, you don't have to travel for thousands of miles to have an adventure-filled holiday. Some of the most beautiful and exciting places on earth are right on your doorstep.

Top Travel Tip

Europe makes an ideal short-haul place to travel around as you don't lose days simply getting there and it has great rail, bus and road links.

Europe

A fantastic example of a European exploration of classic landmarks, kicks off in Amsterdam, where you can whiz along the streets on bikes, visit the Van Gogh Museum and wander along the canals. From here, hop on a train or coach to Paris, for a few days' sightseeing the Louvre, Eiffel Tower, Notre Dame, Arc de Triomphe and street cafes. Moving on, it's a short journey to medieval Lucerne in the Swiss Alps, with its stunning lake and amazing views, followed by a visit to Chamonix, at the foot of Mont Blanc, where you can take a cable car for amazing views of the Alps and enjoy mountain walks. Heading south, take a few days to live it up in the French Riviera, playground of the rich and famous. Have a go at gambling in Monaco or dine on the Promenade at Nice. The final leg of the adventure takes place just across the Spanish border in Barcelona, one of Europe's coolest cities. This is an incredible amount to fit into a few weeks and proves you don't need to be away for six months to get the backpacker experience. Trips like this European example are offered by www.contiki.co.uk, a tour operator offering cheap and exciting holiday experiences for those aged 18–35.

India

If you want to go further afield, India is a great choice as it offers so much instantly and is only a nine-hour flight away. There's something jaw-dropping at every turn and if you plan your route right you can break the back of this vast continent in a month. An ideal tour would take in the key places such as Delhi, Taj Mahal, Varanasi, Khajuraho temples; then Ajanta and Ellora caves, a backwater cruise in Alleppey, Jaipur, Udaipur, Ranthambore for tiger spotting and even a spot of sunbathing on the white sand beaches of Lakshadweep. If you've got the cash, it's a good idea to tailor-make your holiday through a company such as www.indialine.com, as they'll be able to advise you on how to make the most of your time and ensure you see the best the continent has to offer.

South America

South America is a popular choice for gap year travellers, but it's also a fantastic destination for those that have less time on their hands. A really exciting option if you have six weeks available for travel, is the Southern Cross – a 45-day route from Rio to Lima. This awesome trip covers Brazil, Bolivia and Peru and ticks off all the must-see backpacker sights, like Iguasu Falls, Pantanal's wetlands, the isolated Salt Lakes at Uyuni and Nazca Lines. At Lake Titicaca you can experience real Peruvian life in a homestay before embarking on the Inca Trail. This type of short South America trip, packed with adventures, can be booked through www.statravel.co.uk/.

WHICH TRANSPORT?

Sometimes the journey itself can be the best part of travelling, and this is particularly true if you don't have much time – you may as well make the trip part of your holiday!

Boat

If you're after an authentic and adventurous holiday this year, Lake Malawi in Africa is a good option. It's the size of Ireland and borders three countries, plus it has sandy beaches and some of the world's rarest fish. Rather than book into a rustic hotel on its shores for a week, instead become a passenger on the *MV Ilala*, a cargo ship that circuits the lake every week from Monkey Bay, where there's a tiny airport. It ferries around passengers and produce to Malawi, Tanzania and Mozambique and, if you're worried about sleeping conditions, book one of four private cabins. There's also a dining room and sundeck. Ask www.malawi-travel.com for bookings.

Italy offers some of the best boating journeys in the world. Particularly special is a two-week self-cruise starting from Porto Levante, enjoying wildlife in the Po Delta national park, then taking in Chioggia to barter at the famous fish market before heading into Venice for some art and culture. The tiny islands around Venice, such as Murano, Burano and Torcello are magical, as are the lush green landscapes and sandy beaches that line the route to the end destination of Casier. Log on to www.emeraldstar.ie for more European boating ideas.

If you long to make a voyage like great explorers such as Shackleton, but don't have a 19th-century adventurer's holiday allowance, don't despair. There are some trip-of-a-lifetime Antarctica expeditions around, which cram everything into under three weeks, although be warned, they can be pretty costly. An excellent itinerary starts at the Falkland Islands, east of Patagonia, which are home to an astonishing and very tame diversity of wildlife. From here, cruise to South Georgia, a harsher landscape with 7,000ft (2,133m) towering mountains, glaciers and beaches and the resting place of Shackleton. It's also home to millions of king and gentoo penguin colonies, albatross and elephant seals. A cruise south will then bring you to Antarctica, the magical white continent, which is quickly disappearing.

Top Travel Tip

Antarctica trips of various times and prices can be found at www.steppestravel.co.uk.

Car

The Alaska Highway is around 1,500 miles (2,400km) and takes in unbelievably beautiful scenery. It was built in the Second World War to get troops and supplies to Alaska to fight a possible Japanese invasion and is incredibly remote in parts. As you whiz along, you're likely to see bears, moose and maybe even lynx. The scenery en route – which includes Dawson Creek, British Columbia, Yukon Territory, Delta Junction, Fairbanks and Alaska – is sensational. This fantastic trip can be completed between seven to 10 days, but allow longer if you want to stop off a lot on the way.

The Savannah Way is a new 2,300-mile (3,700km) road which spans from Cairns, in Queensland on Australia's east coast, to the historic pearling town of Broom on the west coast. The route takes in 15 national parks, including Kakadu. You'll also see five UNESCO World Heritage sites, including the spectacular Bungle Bungle rock formations in Purnululu National Park, salt pans, the world's longest volcanic tubes, hot springs and mile upon mile of sun-baked landscape. If you barely stopped driving, you could probably complete this in around three days, however, 10 days is a more fun estimate. Plan your trip, including 4x4 hire, at www.savannahway.com.au.

Travelling across Africa from north to south may be a bit ambitious if you've only got a couple of weeks to spare, not to mention dangerous in places. However, a coast-to-coast drive in South Africa is perfect for a short, action-packed break. It's 1,100 miles (1,770km) from Richard's Bay on the southeast coast overlooking the Indian Ocean to Cape Town on the Atlantic west side. As you make your way on the journey, you'll get to experience KwaZulu Natal, the majestic Drakensburg Mountains, wine tasting in the vineyards of Stellenbosh and the famed Garden Route.

Rail

The Trans-Siberian railway is a fantastic experience and takes in some of the most exciting destinations on earth, so there's no way you won't feel as if you've had a true travel experience. Highlights include Moscow, Irkutsk, Lake Baikal, Beijing and the Great Wall of China. You'll need to purchase flights to Moscow and return fares from Beijing and find hotel accommodation at either end; there are four- and two-berth cabins available on the train and the trip takes around 13–16 days, depending on how much time you want to spend in the cities at either end. For more information log on to www.trans-siberia.com.

The California Zephyr is one of the world's great train journeys, going from Chicago to San Francisco by way of America's heartland and the high plains of Colorado, then climbing into the Rocky Mountains via the Oregon Trail. Pioneers came this way, as did gold prospectors and America's first continental telegraph. After Salt Lake City, you cross Bonneville Salt Flats and the beautiful Sierra Nevada. Visit www.amtrak.com for more information.

Checklist

* How long do you have for your holiday?   ☑
* Where to go, Europe or further afield?   ☑
* Get planning your route   ☑
* Which form of transport?   ☑

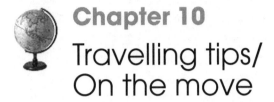

Chapter 10
Travelling tips/
On the move

Travelling from country to country or exploring one destination is all part of the wonderful adventure and can provide some of the best experiences. Driving down a rickety road and turning a corner to reveal one of the world's most beautiful beaches or getting into an animated conversation with a fascinating foreigner on a long rail ride are all memories to be stored away and treasured. However, it's not all Michael Palin-style grand journeys; some travel can be tiring, complicated and, dare I say, a bit boring. So here are some tips on how to make travel fly by with ease.

FLYING

I will provide some tips on how to overcome a fear of flying in Chapter 15, so if this is a concern refer to there. Chances are you're going to be taking at least a couple of flights during your travels, and this can take its toll on you, particularly if they're long-haul.

First of all, get to the airport early. The thought of missing a flight, or actually missing one, is really stressful and is an unnecessary headache that you can easily avoid. Also, by getting to the airport early, you've more chance of getting a seat that you want if you haven't already pre-booked (most airlines now allow you to do this for long-haul flights over the phone or online). The best seats in economy are usually bulkhead (the areas that separate a plane into different sections) as they often have double the leg room of a normal plane seat, plus there's no one in front to recline into you. After bulkhead, I prefer a window seat, not only for the amazing views, but also because it's an extra wall to lean against when you want to get some kip. Emergency exit seats can also offer more leg room, though you have to be prepared to man the doors in a disaster!

Before you check in your luggage, make it distinguishable from others, such as tying a ribbon around the handle or putting a large sticker on it. This will make it much easier to spot at the other end or for others to find it if it gets lost en route. Make sure you buy padlocks for your luggage too, as theft by baggage handlers isn't unknown at airports, and remove any previous travel tags as you don't want any confusion about where your bags should be flying to.

Plane food isn't known for its deliciousness, but you'll still get hungry on a long-haul so if you're vegetarian, or have special dietary requirements, you should let your operator or airline know before you fly. There's usually a choice of dishes, such as fish or chicken, but not always a veggie option, so you do need to order in advance. Alternatively, bring some snacks of your own. I always take a 2-litre (3½ pints) bottle of water on board, as the tiny glasses of water supplied by most airlines aren't enough to keep anyone properly hydrated.

Which leads me on to alcohol and flying. Beauty and travel editors always say you shouldn't drink on flights as it dehydrates you, is bad for the skin and all manner of things. However, I find that on a 19-hour flight, for example, lack of sleep has a far worse effect on me than any alcohol, and a glass or two of red wine actually helps me to snooze. Everyone is different, but I'd say that in moderation, the odd glass isn't going to ruin your flight and will quite possibly help you relax and enjoy it more.

For long-haul flights, you won't regret buying an inflatable neck rest; the tiny pillows most airlines provide are just not comfortable enough to aid sleep so you'll really appreciate it.

Top Travel Tip

Pop some earplugs and an eye mask into your hand luggage, they really do help you to nod off.

I will talk about how to avoid DVT in Chapter 15, and that it's important to regularly stretch and walk around the plane. You need to get the blood circulating in your legs as the cramped conditions of plane seats can make it painful in your knees and cause stiffness in your legs. Remove your footwear when you get on the plane and put on some flight socks, as feet tend to swell in cabin conditions.

Don't forget to pack some entertainment, as you may have watched the films that the airline is playing or, as has been the case on some flights I've been on, there's only one film choice and it's in another language! Books, newspapers, magazines will all help break the monotony of the flight, as will an MP3 player loaded with your favourite tunes, photographs or aural books; even better is a laptop with uploaded films and some headphones. Remember to fully charge any of your electrical items before you fly; there's nothing more annoying than batteries running out halfway through a flight.

Jet lag is for many an inevitable consequence of long-haul travel, particularly if you're travelling west to east. When your body clock is upset, it can result in lethargy and a spaced-out feeling. Everyone has different ways of dealing with it. I find that by immediately adapting to a new country's schedule, I beat jet lag pretty quickly. For example, if I arrive in Bali at noon, I'll try staying awake until at least 9 or 10pm (Bali time) even if I'm beyond tired, so when I wake up the next day I'm already in sync with their time. On the flight, however, I wouldn't try and stop myself sleeping if I'm tired. It's better to arrive somewhere feeling refreshed, whatever time of day it is.

Top Travel Tip

Set your watch to the time of the destination you're travelling to (the pilot usually tells you), so you won't be confused when you land.

If you wear contact lenses, remove them when you get on the plane, as the air conditioning will dry your eyes and it's much easier to get to sleep without them in. As most airlines still don't like you to carry a large amount of liquid in your hand luggage, I put contact lens solution in my lens case prior to travel, which is a small enough amount of liquid to get through security.

Dress comfortably for long-haul flights; anything tight is going to be restricting so opt for loose-fitting t-shirts or sweatshirts in soft materials. I always take a pashmina too, as the air conditioning on flights can get really cold, and they're great to wrap around you and snuggle under like a blanket.

Finally, when you land and collect your luggage, do inspect it before you leave the airport. If the luggage has been damaged in any way, now is the time to go to the airline desk and report it.

RAIL

Train is a fantastic way to travel. Not only is it greener than flying (see Chapter 11) it's also more civilised. Unlike driving, where you have to watch the road, or sitting miles up in the sky in a plane, on a train you can concentrate on the amazing scenery that unfolds as you pass by, so you really do get to see a country properly.

Some of the many benefits of train travel are that it's usually a very cheap way to travel, particularly in the developing world; it won't give you jet lag; you can talk to your friends; read a book or newspaper; have a snooze. There's also a dining car on most trains, which is far better quality than most airline food, plus a bar, which is a great place to meet fellow travellers. It's also a good option if you have a real fear of flying.

You usually need a ticket prior to boarding the train; in some countries getting on without a valid ticket can result in a fine, on other routes you might be able to purchase on board, but it's not worth taking the risk. It's also likely that your ticket price will be a lot cheaper if you book well in advance; as a rule the further ahead you book, particularly at off-peak times, the better value your ticket. I've provided some information about booking rail tickets online in Chapter 3, but if you're buying abroad at the station I'd highly recommend asking someone who knows what they're doing to guide you through the process (ask a fellow traveller who knows the ropes a couple of days before to help you out). You don't want to be queuing for hours only to find out that you're at the wrong window!

As with flights, arrive early as you don't want to miss your train and will want to get a good seat, preferably next to a window so you can watch the scenery unfold. Unless you're on a really low budget, don't opt for third class; in fact you may be amazed at how cheap first class is in some countries, so it's worth enquiring about as it will make your journey much more pleasurable.

Once on board, I'd recommend introducing yourself to your neighbour. You're going to be together for hours if not days, and it's a great way to learn more about a different culture and lifestyle rather than reading about it from a guidebook. Talking is a great way to pass the time and you may gain a friend.

Top Travel Tip

Travelling overnight on a train is a good way to save money on hostel or hotel accommodation.

The reclining seats found in most modern standard carriages make it easy to sleep in comfort – something that is almost impossible on a crowded airplane or bus, let alone in a car. It's a good idea to take a blanket or light sleeping bag in case the air conditioning becomes too much, and choose a seat away from the doors. On some trains there are sleeping compartments, ranging from singles up to family size; these usually need to be booked in advance. You get extra privacy and facilities (sometimes including a free evening meal), bed linen and blankets are provided, and usually complimentary tea or coffee in the morning.

VEHICLES

Great road trips, as mentioned in Chapter 11, can be immensely exciting. While plane and train are great for getting you from A to B quickly, sometimes it's nice to go to C and D too, and you can if you're in a car as you're completely in control. It also means you can go to exactly the destination you want to, not 200 miles (320 km) south of it as is often the case with a plane. Plus you can make stops as and when you want, so if you see something interesting you can go and discover it there and then.

Before you can get booking a road trip, you'll need to have all the necessary documents. For starters, your British driving licence may not be accepted in some countries, so you'll need to invest in an International Driving Permit (IDP), which you can apply for through the AA (www.theaa.com). It lasts for up to 12 months from the date of issue and allows you to drive a private vehicle along with a valid UK licence.

There are all sorts of devices to help you plan your route, as well as traditional maps. Satellite Navigation (SatNav) is a useful tool for your car as it can locate you and your destination and find you the quickest or most scenic way to arrive there. More advanced models can also point out places of historic interest, restaurants and hotels en route. I've used one across the length of France and found it invaluable for tracking down bargain places to stay when you're too tired to drive another mile. There are also route planners on sites such as AA (www.theaa.com) and RAC (www.rac.co.uk), which provide maps and written instructions, which you can print out.

You may be interested in hiring a car once you reach a destination, Fly-Drive as it's been nicknamed, (see Chapter 9 for hire companies), or some travellers purchase a car at the start of their journey and sell it at the end. If you're going to do this, it's best to have at least some idea of what a reliable, functioning car should look like, including the engine. Before you go, ask a mechanically minded friend to give you the low down. Be sure to take the car for a test drive before you part with any money and don't tell the seller that you're going on a road trip (so won't be able to come back if anything goes wrong) as you'll be less likely to be ripped off.

Top Travel Tip

Don't leave lots of valuables on show in your car, lock them in the boot. It's easy to forget when you're relaxed and on holiday that the same rules apply the world over and that a car stuffed with goodies is rich pickings for an opportunist thief.

Campervans are a fun option to a car. The benefits being that you've got your bed, kitchen and toilet on site, so there's no need for budget-sapping hotels or restaurants. The downside is that they're usually slower than cars, eat up more petrol and cost more to hire or buy.

BOATS

I've offered boats as an option for green travel in Chapter 11 such as freight ships, or as an option for an amazing short break journey in Chapter 9, but here I'm going to give some tips on how to make boat travel safer and more pleasurable.

For a start, travel by boat is a charming alternative to flying, but it can be very slow. If you're on a boat for a considerable amount of time, there is the possibility of seasickness, which can ruin a trip. If you know that you suffer from this or are worried about the possibility, then pack some anti-seasickness tablets. I'd also recommend staying in the centre of the ship if possible, fixing your eyes on the horizon and avoiding too much food and drink. As a rule, smaller boats are worse than larger ones for causing seasickness.

Whether you're taking a tiny ferry from island to island in the tropics or cruising around the Caribbean in a massive liner, it's important to have a quick health and safety check before setting sail. Make sure there are lifejackets on board, and if you can't see any, ask where they are; ditto life rafts if it's a larger boat. If the people in charge are trying to cram too many people (and animals as is sometimes the case!) onto a ferry and you're getting concerned, simply get off and get the next one; it's not worth the worry. Some of boats that have been overloaded in the developing world have proved to be death traps.

BUSES

Backpackers tend to love buses as they're one of the cheapest ways to travel, you get to meet the locals up close and personal and it's much greener than taking a plane.

It's great as a method of getting from village to village or town to town in a destination, but check with someone, such as fellow travellers or hostel staff, when the buses run. You don't want to be standing at a stop for hours only to find out there's only one bus a day! Be prepared for a far more colourful, noisy and entertaining bus journey than you may be used to at home. In some countries, such as India, a lot tends to get squeezed on to a bus, along with tightly packed people, it's not unusual to be sharing a seat or passageway with chickens, sacks of fruit and veg or bales of hay. This can be charming if you're only travelling for a short distance, but can become annoying if your journey is a very long one!

The cons of bus travel are that they can be unreliable, in terms of pick-up times and also break downs. The road conditions in some countries are also pretty poor; a journey spent bumping around in your seat for hours can become quite uncomfortable. There's often no air conditioning on buses, just the windows for ventilation, so it can get incredibly hot on board which can lead to feelings of nausea, as can continual winding roads. Make sure you take plenty of water with you infused with ginger, which can help alleviate sickness.

Try to avoid travelling on buses alone at night. Chances are you'll be fine, but there's more risk of theft (try to keep your luggage close by you at all times rather than allowing someone to put it in a compartment above you), and unlit roads are more dangerous to drive along in the evening.

MOTORBIKES/BICYCLES

In some places, such as Amsterdam or Beijing, the bicycle rules. However, in the majority of places they don't, so while it's a fantastic way to get about, you'll need to be extra cautious when you're on two wheels.

If you are hankering after the idea of feeling the wind in your hair on a motorbike, then there are a few things to consider. In many parts of the world you may be able to hire out, or even buy, a motorbike without having to show a valid driving licence. This may seem like a blessing while you are travelling, but in reality it can endanger both yourself and others. So, you need to make sure that you have a full driving licence before leaving home. In the UK, anyone aged 16 and over can take the driving theory test to ride a moped, but a valid provisional licence (aged 17 and over) must be obtained for completing the Compulsory Basic Training (CBT) and road test for a full driving licence, including motorbikes. In addition to a valid licence from the UK, some countries may also require you to hold an International Driving Permit (IDP) before you can legally drive there (see Vehicles section of this chapter).

You'll also need motorbike insurance, which can be purchased separately or your travel insurance may cover you for dangerous sporting activities including motorcycle hire. Unfortunately, motorbikes have a higher rate of injury associated with them than cars, so make sure you also have proper medical insurance and that it's valid overseas.

Before driving a motorbike in any country make sure that you read up on the rules of the road, such as which side of the road you're meant to be riding. Also remember that any sort of driving under the influence of alcohol or drugs should be avoided, that driving when you're tired or jet lagged is inadvisable, and that wearing a proper helmet and gear while riding a motorbike is essential.

Top Travel Tip

Check with the embassy or consulate of the country in which you will be driving so you can begin to learn local rules of the road before you leave home.

Cycling is a fun option that you may not have considered. Once you've got your hands on a bicycle not only is travel free, it also allows you to get to really off-the-beaten-track places that public transport may not reach. Many travellers find that they need to get around during their travels but bikes are particularly relevant to travellers who are staying in one place for a little while, such as voluntary placements, who find that bicycles are cheap, require little maintenance and allow them to travel quickly wherever they need.

If you're planning on buying a bike while you're away, look for safety aspects first; tyres should still have some tread and be fully inflated, metal parts shouldn't be rusty or broken and the seat should have springs or some padding. A lock is essential if you don't want your bike to get stolen, so try asking for one as part of the deal. A helmet is also a must.

If you're going to be taking your kit with you when you cycle, it's essential to buy as much lightweight stuff as you can as cycling with a heavy rucksack can be seriously hard work. Make sure you've got a repair kit and plenty of water with you wherever you go to avoid problems.

Top Travel Tip

Try to avoid cycling in the heat of the midday sun – take a siesta and get back on the road in the afternoon to avoid sunstroke.

Join up to the Cycling Touring Club, (CTC) www.ctc.org.uk, before you go. For £36 per year, you get loads of benefits including money off clothing, bikes and ferries. Plus it helps you plot cycling routes worldwide, has a friendly forum where you can get advice from other cyclists, has a great online shop to boost your kit and features holiday and touring suggestions.

Checklist

* Get to the airport/station early; book your
  seats in advance if possible   ☑
* Take water, an inflatable neck rest and
  some entertainment on board an aircraft   ☑
* Inspect your luggage at the arrival point   ☑
* Take an overnight train to save money on
  accommodation   ☑
* Check you have a correct driving licence
  for road trips   ☑
* Check for safety measures on all boats   ☑
* Try to avoid bus travel at night   ☑
* Keep cycle kit as light as possible   ☑
* Invest in safety gear such as a helmet   ☑

Chapter 11
Going green

From the constant bombardment of information about the state of the planet from scientists, television programmes and newspapers for the past five years, you'll be aware that there's a green movement going on. There's no denying that travel is a contributor to greater carbon emissions, which ultimately leads to climate change. And it's not just planes that increase your carbon footprint; it's the taxi that you jump into on arrival, the hotel you check into with air conditioning and 24-hour laundry service; the fire you sit around on the beach; even the plastic spoon you use to stir your drink.

Okay, this all may sound like I'm trying to prevent you from having fun overseas. I'm not, as realistically I know you'll probably still travel, but I do think that we all have a responsibility to try and be as green as we can while we're taking a trip. If you're going to use the planet as your playground, the very least you can do is try and tidy up as you go!

HOW CAN I MAKE MY JOURNEY GREENER?

Carbon offsetting
First off, carbon offsetting doesn't mean that you can conveniently forget what harm you're doing to the environment by flying around the world. The bottom line is that we all need to

fly less. However, the likelihood is that you are going to take at least a couple of flights for your trip, so one option at least to try to counterbalance the damage is carbon offsetting. This means calculating your carbon emissions from the length of time you'll be flying and converting that into to monetary total.

For example, if you're travelling from London Heathrow Airport to Bangkok in Thailand, you would be creating around 4.37 tonnes of carbon dioxide. To then offset this much carbon, you could opt for a scheme such as providing low-energy lighting in Africa, which costs £9.50 per tonne, so your grand total would be £41.50.

It might look complicated at first glance, but there are plenty of companies available to help you calculate your emissions quickly and simply and which then give you the option to put this sum towards a green scheme, such as tree planting or solar ovens. There are lots of websites offering a quick calculation service, such as www.co2balance.uk.com, www.carbonneutral.com, www.climatecare.org and www.carbonfootprint.com.

Top Travel Tip

Some airlines, such as EasyJet and British Airways, actually provide a carbon offsetting option when you book, though be warned it's unlikely that the airline will be contributing as much as an independent scheme.

There's currently an ongoing debate about how beneficial carbon offsetting is for the environment. The idea that we can cancel out our own greenhouse gases by paying for projects that reduce the gases elsewhere is seen by some as too convenient; a way to lessen guilt for Westerners by allowing them to travel as much they like without ultimately taking responsibility. There is also a shadow cast over the reliability of some of the schemes, although the companies provided above are a safe bet.

Personally, I offset carbon because I think it's better to do something than nothing. I have to travel for my job and if someone elsewhere in the world benefits every time I fly, this is a better option to me than simply taking a plane.

Ironically, the fact that more people than ever before are jetting off around the world has also seen some benefits to the environment. The positive effects of tourism include the preservation of rainforests and protecting animals close to extinction. Without the tourist draw, and revenue, animals such as the elephant or rhino, for example, would almost certainly be teetering on the brink of extinction in Africa. People are realising that an animal is far more valuable alive if it brings in eco tourists willing to pay thousands of pounds to photograph it.

Alternative transport

You don't have to fly! If you're going travelling for a long period of time, you have the luxury of opting for greener modes of transport to get around. Travelling by train is a good alternative. Eurostar (www.eurostar.com) claims that it generates ten times less carbon dioxide (CO_2) than planes that fly the same routes, such as London to Paris, which generates 122kg (269lb) of CO_2 by train, but 168kg (370lb) of CO_2 by plane. For more rail options, refer to Chapter 10.

Travelling by boat is a trickier issue than you might think. You'd assume it's a naturally greener option than a carbon-belching plane, but experts reckon that some cruise ships actually emit more toxins into the world than are caused by flying. Most ships don't have carbon offset schemes, yet larger vessels create a lot of CO_2, plus they're often guilty of dumping waste in the sea, not to mention cruising to islands that aren't properly equipped to cope with the ship or the hordes of tourists disembarking each day. However, the culprits are mainly the large cruise operators; hopping aboard a small riverboat, where you wouldn't be allowed to throw so much as an apple peel over the side, for a journey along the Amazon is a different story. The most environmentally friendly option is a sailing ship. Check out companies such as www.gapadventures.com, which offers a tall ship trip along the coastline of Brazil. Also consider the slow boat option and book a trip on a cargo ship. Ships are ferrying around freight all over the world's seas every day, so it makes perfect sense to hitch a ride on one. While it won't be the most luxurious accommodation you'll have stayed in, some ships do have extras like a bar or DVD library to help pass the time. Take a look at Strand Voyages (www.strandtravel.co.uk), which specialises in providing voyages on cargo ships, or try www.freightertrips.com.

Environmentalists seem to differ as to how bad travelling by car is compared to plane. Suffice to say, if you take one journey and work out the CO_2 emissions for all major forms of transport, the worst culprit appears to be plane, followed by car, bus, train. Of course there are lots of factors to be taken into consideration. If there are four of you in a fuel-efficient car, this is obviously better than going on a solo trip in a 4x4. If you're planning on a great road journey, there are a few tips to keep your green halo shining. First off, rent a fuel-efficient car. It's actually really easy these days as most of the major rental firms like Hertz (www.hertz.co.uk) and Avis (www.avis.co.uk) have hybrids such as the Toyota Prius on offer. If you can't get one of those, then opt for a small, compact car, which will use a lot less petrol (and cost you less too). Plan your route carefully (or make sure the car has SatNav), as getting lost and driving miles out of your way wastes precious petrol.

Top Travel Tip

Cruising at a gentle speed, such as 50 or 60mph (80–90kph) rather than pushing the car to its limit, is likely to save hundreds of gallons of fuel on a long road trip.

Taking public transport rather than getting around privately wherever you go is a great way to reduce your carbon footprint. If you've got the time, take buses for overland trips. In cities, hop in a human-powered rickshaw rather than a taxi, it's carbon neutral, or take a metro if available. Exploring a destination by bike is cheap, green and most of all fun, plus you're keeping fit too. In cities such as Amsterdam and Beijing, bikes actually rule the streets so it makes sense to hire one while you're there. Some travellers base their whole trip around bike journeys and independent tour operators like Intrepid Travel (www.intrepidtravel.com) offer global cycling tours.

And of course the humble foot is a great, and green, mode of transport. A walking trip, whether it's trekking the Inca trail or climbing Mount Kilimanjaro, has many benefits, from health to interacting with the environment. Of course, you may have taken a plane to reach your destination, which is detrimental to the environment and means that your trip isn't truly green, plus some argue that large numbers of walkers can be damaging to the environment, particularly if they leave debris such as plastic water bottles.

Top Travel Tip

For more ideas on ways to make your journeys more eco-friendly, log on to www.ecotravelling.co.uk, which has lots of information on different types of transport and planning advice.

STAYING GREEN

One of the best ways of doing your bit for the environment while you're away is by staying in eco or green accommodation. Hotels are responsible for a huge drain on energy resources, from 24/7 air conditioning, heating and lighting, to mass usage of lots of non-degradable products, like plastic spoons and shampoo bottles.

Booking directly, if possible, guarantees that profits go straight to the hotel or lodge. However, there are some tour operators in the UK that deal in ethical travel and are concerned with conservation, local cultures and ensuring your travel footprint is as light as possible.

Top Travel Tip

Responsible Travel (www.responsibletravel.com), which is geared towards travel that benefits local people, has an excellent range of eco lodges all over the world, from rainforests in Costa Rica to Thailand's beaches.

Eco Hotels of the World (www.ecohotelsoftheworld.com), is independent and offers information on some of the greenest places to stay on the planet. Hotels can't pay to be on the site and it doesn't accept commission on bookings, so you know that the editor's advice really is independent. Eco Hotels has created a rating system, which is split into five categories assessing energy, water, disposal, eco-active and protection, with each being rated from one to five stars.

Be careful, standards of green accommodation vary around the world. It can be quite tricky to establish what's authentic and what's not, particularly if your only information is from a website. The problem is, some hotels are riding the green wave without actually doing anything to lessen their impact on the environment, so in order to be sure it's a truly green establishment, here are a few questions to ask before booking your hotel:

- Is the hotel locally owned and operated? If not, is it at least staffed by local employees?
- What kind of recycling initiatives does the hotel have (aluminium, plastic, paper, grey water, composting)?
- Do guests have the option to reuse towels and sheets instead of having them changed every day?
- What programmes does the hotel have to reduce consumption? Examples include energy-efficient lighting, low-flow toilets and showers, and alternative energy sources like solar or wind power.
- How does the hotel contribute to the local community?

There are some excellent books available on green travel if you want more ideas and information, including Alastair Sawday's *Green Places to Travel*, Earthscan's *Ethical Travel Guide*, Lonely Planet's *Code Green*, AA's *Green Rooms* and Duncan Clark's *The Rough Guide to Ethical Living*.

Green Travel Tips

* Pack as many biodegradable products as possible.
* Take a reusable water filter bottle so you don't have to buy plastic water bottles.
* Help preserve local wildlife and habitats by sticking to regulations; e.g. walk on marked footpaths, don't stand on or break coral and don't buy products made from endangered plants or animals.
* Support the local economy wherever you are; buy local drinks, food and clothing and stay in local accommodation where possible, so you know the money goes directly to the hands of the people.
* Use recycling bins wherever you can.
* Use recyclable batteries for your electrical equipment and pack a solar charger.
* Take organic toiletries which aren't full of chemicals so won't have a harmful effect on the environment. And don't use hotel toiletries, which are usually in wasteful packing.
* Sign up to www.greentraveller.co.uk, which is free and bursting with information on green issues, from eco hotels to transport alternatives to flying, plus there's an active forum.

Checklist

* Carbon offset ☑
* Consider alternative forms of transport to a plane ☑
* Take public transport where possible ☑
* Hire a bicycle at your destination ☑
* Book green or eco accommodation ☑
* Recycle whenever possible ☑
* Use water filters instead of buying bottled water ☑
* Read up on green travel ☑

Chapter 12
Life-changing travel

In a way, all travel changes your life a little, simply by exposing you to new ideas, places and cultures. However, some people set out to change the way they are through travel, from losing weight to trying to find the meaning of life! If you've got a desire to change more than just your socks while you're away, here are a few ideas to help you on your way.

SPIRITUAL

If the words spiritual retreat summon up images of crystals and hippies, think again. More and more everyday Westerners are going to them as the stresses and strains of life continue to become greater. It's not often that you get to spend time with just yourself away from mobile phones, computers and a mountain of paper work, and you might just find that a visit to a retreat is the start of a great personal, and life-changing, journey. At the very least, you're going to come out feeling a lot more calm and relaxed than when you went in!

Ashrams

Ashrams, the majority of which are in India, have long been popular places for Westerners of all ages to head when they're in need of spiritual enlightenment, to heal, trying to find out the meaning of life or simply curious to live in a completely different culture.

There are hundreds of different types of Ashrams in Indian, but overall their aim is to teach residents the art of living, by being spiritually aware and contributing to the social good. Some Ashrams have a live-in guru, while others continue to teach the work of a guru that's passed away. Most places will expect students, or devotees, to contribute to Ashram life in some way while they're there, which could be anything from helping to prepare food to cleaning the toilets, as well studying and meditating.

Most Ashrams are reliant on volunteer work and donations, and charge very little money for food and accommodation, which is usually in a same-sex shared room. Don't go expecting to be living in a hotel; it's not. Accommodation is pretty basic in most places, with shared bathrooms and dining (sometimes men and women are expected to dine separately). However, this shouldn't be viewed simply as a cheap way to travel around India; most people that go are intent on finding out more about Indian philosophy and the art of living, and you'll quickly tire of classes and volunteer work if your heart's not in it. You'll be expected to cover up in loose clothing, although each Ashram has its own dress code.

If you're keen to find out more and visit one, then think about how long you want to go for. Some Ashrams don't mind casual drop-in visitors, provided they have the room, but some will only allow longer stays and proven devotees to visit.

Top Travel Tip

Perhaps the most famous Ashram among Westerners is Amritapuri, in Kerala, where live-in guru Amma is known for hugging during a darshan (meeting her devotees), sometimes up to a thousand in a day! If you want to stay or find out more information visit www.amritapuri.org/ashram, which also lists Amma centres around the world.

Buddhist retreats

Buddhism, a set of beliefs and practices based on the teachings of Siddhartha Gautama, known as Buddha, is popular throughout Asia and the world, with an estimated 250 million-plus devotees.

There are Buddhist retreats around the world, including the UK, and you don't have to be a Buddhist to spend time at them. The reason a trip to a retreat can be life changing is that as well as learning about the philosophy, you're encouraged to find out about yourself too. Sounds a bit hippy dippy? Well it can be, but it's a really fantastic, and healing, travel experience particularly if you're stressed, burnt out or just need a new way of looking at the world.

This isn't a spa-like experience. Much like an Ashram, you'll often be expected to pull your weight while you're there, taking part in everyday chores and sharing a room. If you're staying in a Buddhist monastery, it's also likely that you'll have to take part in the rituals, which can be before dawn; this is hardcore stuff, and not for those that just fancy a bit of a relaxing break.

Top Travel Tip

It's best to start off at a beginner's retreat if you're not au fait with the philosophy. You'll be taught the temple protocols and everything from meditation to classes will be explained. There's sometimes the chance to learn new activities too, from tai chi to kung fu, depending on the type of retreat you've chosen. Also you'll be with other beginners, so it's a good way of meeting other likeminded people.

If you want to find a Buddhist retreat, it can be tricky. For a start there are thousands worldwide, plus they're not all authentic. A good place to start your search, or to find if there's a Buddhist centre or retreat somewhere that you'll be travelling through, try www.buddhanet.info, which lists pretty much every foundation in the world and provides contact details.

HEALTH & WELLBEING

As well as good mental health, it's also important to be in good physical health, and people are increasingly using travel to merge the two, sorting out everything from being overweight to relaxation and lowering blood pressure. It's one of the fastest growing areas in travel today, and for good reason; who doesn't want to come back from holiday glowing with health and with a new regime for living?

Spas

Okay, checking into a spa doesn't sound life changing. However, I'm not talking about having a facial and a manicure a couple of times, I'm talking serious, life-enhancing getaways that aim to change the way you look after yourself as well as the way you look.

Ayurveda spas, which are extremely common in Asia, can be found around the world. Ayurveda is a 5,000-year-old practice, means science of life, and is holistic practice, which means that the whole body is considered when treating a specific ailment or problem. For example, if you are having trouble sleeping, an Ayurvedic doctor won't give you a sleeping pill, they'll look at what you eat, your daily routine and exercise.

On arrival at live-in Ayurvedic spas you'll be analysed and prescribed your Dosha (mind/body type according to natural elements), from which you'll know what foods you should be eating (usually vegetarian) and which you should be avoiding.

As well as preventing and healing diseases and their symptoms, Ayurveda also aims to strengthen the immune system, increase the body's general wellbeing and delay the ageing process. Most Ayurveda centres also offer daily yoga and meditation as part of the programme. Even if you don't have any specific ailments when you arrive, this is a fantastic way to get really fit and healthy in a short space of time, and learn new techniques for living back home.

Top Travel Tip

For a great selection of Ayurveda spas around the world, check out www.bodyandsoulholidays.info, www.nealsyardagency.com and www.wellbeingescapes.co.uk.

Some spas, or wellbeing retreats, offer life coaching, which is ideal if you're at a stage in life where you're feeling confused, under too much pressure, are in a transition period or just want to gain a deeper understanding of what you want from life. Life-coaching trips tend to consist of daily activities, plus individual sessions with a life coach to discuss most aspects of your life, including health, diet, setting goals and managing pressure. The idea is that when you leave, you'll be able to cope better with what life has to throw at you. You might question why you need to travel to find this, and the answer is you don't, but a change of scenery is almost always good for the soul and a great start to help you achieve your goal.

In order to ensure that the life coach is fully trained and reputable, I'd recommend booking your trip through a specialist tour operator, such as www.lotusjourneys.com or a course, such as www.lifecraft.co.uk, which offers life coaching on board a boat.

A beautiful retreat I recently discovered is The Hill That Breathes, www.thehillthatbreathes.com, in Italy, which lies in an Italian farmhouse in 100 acres of woodland close to the Renaissance hill town of Urbino. It offers brilliant programmes, from tai chi to rebirthing, geared towards anyone looking for a serious life change. Some programmes are with famous gurus, such as the Barefoot Doctor, who takes you through Taoism-based techniques for releasing inhibitions and unleashing your inner playful spirit during the course of a week. One of the most popular programmes are the F**k It weeks, aimed at people that have reached the end of their tether trying too hard to make things work in life but getting nowhere. Course leaders claim that people who have said F**k It and headed off to the hills for a week of release have gone home to see their lives transformed, from finding love to finally selling a house that wouldn't budge.

If you're feeling sluggish, permanently tired and want to lose weight but don't feel you can get out of a rut, then a trip to a wellbeing retreat for a detox may well be the solution, plus it's likely to help you keep trim in the long run. The beauty of this type of spa is that you don't just detox and are then sent away, it often involves sessions with nutritionists, exercise experts and holistic massages to get you back on the right road. Depending on what sort of place you choose, this can be challenging or simple. As with all trips of this nature, it's important that you do your research and book with a reputable company to avoid disappointment. In:spa (www.inspa-retreats.com) has a good reputation and offers a selection of detox retreats, ditto Holistic Holidays (www.hoho.co.uk/detox.html).

Yoga

You don't have to be as bendy as a piece of rubber to take part in a yoga holiday, in fact you don't even need to have been practising for years to join in. What you do need is commitment and ideally use it to carry on with what you've learnt back home. Yoga, which in the West we know as a series of often physically demanding positions, is actually a way of life, including body, mind and inner spirit, which has been practised in the east for thousands of years.

There are thousands of courses, holidays and retreats around the world to choose from, but if it's your first introduction to yoga or you don't practise much, then a beginner's getaway would be ideal. You need to decide what you want from the holiday before you start looking; some retreats are quite serious and you're expected to participate in practice at least twice a day, eat vegetarian food and not drink, whereas some specialist tour operators have designed sun and sand holidays with some yoga thrown in. There are lots of reputable companies with a very good standard of teaching; take a look at www.yogatraveller.com, www.yogatravel.co.uk and www.responsibletravel.com.

LEARNING

Life-changing travel of course includes most of the chapters in this book, from volunteering to solo travel, which all help to improve confidence, the way you look at the world and raise self-esteem. However, if you're looking to change your life through the skills that you have rather than the way you think, then you may be considering a trip where you learn as well as discover.

Learning any new activity, such as climbing, salsa dancing, painting or diving, is not only a fantastic feeling but can also give you a new focus and hobby for life. It's also amazing the knock-on effect a new social activity can have; you never know, that handsome bloke you tangoed with may just end up being more than your dancing partner!

Just like wellbeing, this is a booming area in travel, particularly among young women who aren't content to come back from holiday with just a tan any more. A really popular choice is creative writing, where you learn to get going on that novel you've always dreamed of penning, or have an expert tweak what you've already done.

Top Travel Tip

Exclusive Escapes (www.exclusiveescapes.co.uk) offers a critically acclaimed writing course in Turkey, while Creative Escapes (www.creative-escapes.co.uk) offers writing retreats in Morocco and Cambodia, and also photography courses.

A dancing holiday is a great way to give yourself a new lease of life, particularly if you're the sort of person that isn't usually the first one up on a dance floor. Not only does it improve confidence, it also brings you into direct contact with lots of other people, so it's very sociable – perfect if you feel stuck in a social rut – plus it will make you feel fit and healthy and it's a skill that you can continue back home. If you've always wanted to have a go at salsa (pretty much everyone I know would love to be able to salsa!), then have a look at Dance Holidays (www.danceholidays.com), which offers some amazingly hot trips to places such as Cuba, Toronto, Grenada and Barcelona. You'll get two hours of dance classes a day, three- or four-star hotel accommodation, tour host and lots of parties and nights out to practise your new skills! If you don't fancy salsa, there's also tango, flamenco, Bollywood, Latin, swing, ceroc and belly dancing holidays to try. One of the bonuses of Dance Holidays is that they also offer classes and workshops in the UK too, plus lots of social nights so you can enjoy Margaritas and Merengue dancing all year round.

There are loads of travel companies offering more learning holidays, but exercise caution and make sure they're a member of ABTA and IATA to ensure high standards. Why Don't You . . . Live Life to the Full (www.whydontyou.com) is a great one with dozens of ideas, from surf lessons in Brazil to learning to cook in Thailand. STA Travel (www.statravel.co.uk) also has lots of exciting, and cheap, options for students or those under 26.

Checklist

* Look at spiritual retreats if you're feeling stressed/lost ☑
* Consider volunteering at an Ashram ☑
* Look into Buddhist retreats ☑
* Ayurveda spas for health and wellbeing ☑
* Yoga if you're looking to improve mind and body ☑
* Creative writing escapes ☑
* Dancing to improve confidence and skills ☑
* Investigate more learning experiences ☑

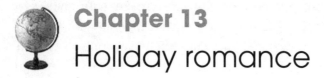

Chapter 13
Holiday romance

You're young, free and (possibly) single and it's pretty likely that while you're trotting around the globe you're going to meet other people like yourself, some of whom you're likely to want to be more than friends with.

Holiday romances can be fantastic. Having a great time in an exotic country with an exciting new stranger is heady stuff and will hopefully be full of memories you'll treasure forever. Plus there's the added benefit that if it works out, great, if it doesn't you can move on to the next destination or are safe in the knowledge that you'll never have to see them again when you head home!

TO FLING OR NOT TO FLING?

The majority of holiday flings are just that; happy, light-hearted and short-lasting. However, some couples simply fall in love and change their lives so that they can be together. This is heart-warming stuff and ideal if you're the secure type who just wants a bit of fun. However, if you're the sort of person who tends to get heavily involved in relationships early on, or who's feeing emotionally vulnerable, then it's not always wise to get involved with someone while you're away. It might feel at the time that you're living in the moment, but if it's going to make you really upset when it's time to part (whether that's after a couple of nights or a couple of months) or even cause you to return home, then it's not worth getting involved. If this sounds like you, then I'd recommend staying away from the person or moving on as quickly as possible! Of course, if you think you've met your future husband then go for it, but if you're confusing lust and love then be wary.

SAFETY

Holiday flings aren't all Mills & Boon stuff about heartbreak and romance; they can actually be dangerous if you don't take precautions.

Con artists

For starters, you have to be very careful about who you're seeing. Do you really know the person? Conmen operate in resorts all over the world, from backpacker getaways to five-star hotels. Every year the Foreign & Commonwealth Office hears cases of women who have been robbed by men that have wormed their way into their affections. This is a very hard theft to prove and many women don't even want to report it, as they feel embarrassed to have fallen for a trickster's charms. Don't feel stupid, it's vital that it gets reported in order for this sort of guy to be stopped.

How can you spot a conman? Well it's tricky, but as a rule, things to look out for are if someone is continually asking you for money (not just the odd drink, but always losing their wallet at dinner or for a loan to tide them over), and talking about themselves in a self-aggrandizing fashion, bragging about their larger-than-life accomplishments and schemes, which are often completely fabricated. Also be wary if they try to keep you from your friends or from meeting theirs; what have they got to hide?

Drugs & alcohol

There's an increased use of drugs to spike drinks and food around the world in tourist hot spots. Known as date-rape drugs, even though they're often used simply to rob people while they're unconscious, the two drugs that are mainly used are GHB, gamma-hydroxybutyric acid, and Rohypnol. Scarily, GHB has very similar effects to being really drunk, plus it's invisible when dissolved and doesn't smell, so some people aren't even aware they've been drugged. Rohypnol acts as a sedative and can make you start feeling drowsy after around 20 minutes and usually lasts around eight hours. If you think you've been a victim of a date-rape drug, it's essential that you get yourself to a police station as quickly as possible to report the crime and also for a drugs test – waiting too long to test for the presence of drugs may be detrimental because these type of drugs are quickly metabolised and eliminated by the body.

Top Travel Tip

Be really careful about accepting drinks from strangers in restaurants, bars and clubs. It may be really flattering at the time, not to mention save you money, but you could be risking your safety.

Date-rape drugs sound scary, but it's actually alcohol-related incidents that are far more frequent with travellers. If you've consumed large quantities of booze then you're vulnerable, particularly if you're in a foreign country where Western women are viewed as 'easy' compared to local women. The best advice is not to get into a state where you can't function properly or have trouble remembering. It's not about not having a good time, it's about not putting yourself at risk of rape, assault or theft.

Rape & sexual assault

The best advice on rape and sexual assault is to avoid being in a position where it's possible, and to be as vigilant as you would at home. This includes turning down drinks from strangers; watching your alcohol content; not walking alone at night in quiet areas, in particular beaches and parks; avoiding quiet carriages on trains and buses at night if possible; taking registered taxis; locking your accommodation doors and windows at night if possible; and abiding by local laws and customs, such as covering up and wearing modest clothing in Muslim countries.

Of course, following these suggestions doesn't mean that it's not going to happen – sadly some attacks happen in broad daylight even in busy areas – but by taking notice of them you put yourself at less risk. If you are a victim of a sexual assault while away, you should tell the relevant embassy as soon as possible, a full list of which are in Chapter 16. You should also tell the local police station as soon as possible and insist on a police report.

The Foreign & Commonwealth Office (www.fco.gov.uk) says that, if you get in touch with the UK embassy or consulate in the country where the attack took place (or the nearest one if there isn't one in the destination), it can help with the following: telling you about local police and legal procedures; accompanying you to the local police station and where possible try to ensure you are interviewed by a female officer; provide a list of local lawyers and interpreters; help you to deal with the local authorities in arranging a medical examination where possible with a female doctor; depending on local laws and customs it can also arrange for you to get advice on sexually transmitted infections, and on pregnancy and abortion; contact relatives or friends if needed and to provide information on what professional help is available locally and back in the UK.

HEALTH

If you're going to be sleeping with someone while you're travelling, the same rules apply as they do at home; unless you know a person's full sexual history, and trust them, take precautions.

And by precautions I don't just mean contraception against pregnancy, like the Pill or coil, I mean precaution against sexual diseases. The best way to stay safe while you're away is to use condoms. There's no excuse not to take them, they're free from family planning clinics all over the UK (www.fpa.org.uk), there are no side effects, it protects you and the person you're sleeping with and they're 95 per cent effective against pregnancy.

It's unlikely that the guy is always going to have contraceptives on him and if you've got some to hand you'll be less likely to be naughty and not use any precautions. Some women don't like the idea of carrying lots of condoms with them and would rather buy them as they go. If this is the case with you be aware that if you're travelling or volunteering in the third world it can actually be very hard to buy condoms. Always make sure that they carry the British kite mark or European CE mark as that means they've been tested to a strict safety standard.

Top Travel Tip

Rubber perishes with heat and age, so if you've been carrying condoms around for a long time and they've become brittle or discoloured, it's time to ditch them and buy some more.

Sexually Transmitted Infections are one of the real risks of a holiday fling and can cast a cloud over your whole trip if you don't take precautions. There are some STIs which, while painful and irritating, aren't harmful and can be treated fairly easily, providing you're in a country with good medical facilities. These include: chlamydia, which can be treated with antibiotics; genital warts, which can be frozen off with nitrogen (although there's no cure yet for relapses); gonorrhoea, which can be treated with antibiotics; pelvic inflammatory diseases, which can also be treated with antibiotics; trichomonas, which can be treated with antiparasitics and antibiotics.

However, there are some STIs which can be more life threatening such as hepatitis B, which it's estimated around 2 billion people have been infected with worldwide, 400 million chronically. It causes (sometimes chronic and ultimately fatal) inflammation of the liver. It's commonly spread through body fluids (like saliva, sharing a toothbrush) and sharing drug equipment like needles.

If the worst does happen and you find yourself with an STI while abroad, don't panic. Most STIs are treatable, provided you begin treatment as soon as possible, and the most uncomfortable symptoms can usually be cleared up fairly quickly. If you notice, or feel, anything unusual after having sex see a doctor immediately. And for real peace of mind, get yourself checked out when you come back from a trip if you've been sexually active, as some STIs can go unnoticed for weeks before symptoms occur.

HIV/AIDS

It's estimated that around 38 million people have Human Immuno-deficiency Virus (HIV) which results in Acquired Immune Deficiency Syndrome (AIDS), which causes millions of deaths each year. The virus attacks your white blood cells reducing the body's ability to fight infections and cancer. It can be caught in several ways, including sharing needles (which can be tattooing, not just drugs, so think twice before getting one done when you're away), and through unprotected sex. At first the symptoms are indistinguishable from any other virus; sore throat and joint pains, or there won't be any symptoms at all. The carrier can have it for years without being aware, so you also have to consider using contraception if you've been sexually active and never had an HIV test – it's not just you that you're protecting, but others too.

There are HIV/AIDS hot spots that you should be aware of. Africa in particular suffers from widespread infection, with Swaziland, Botswana, Lesotho, Zimbabwe, South Africa, Namibia, Malawi, Nigeria, Mozambique and Tanzania all with high prevalence of the virus. If you're going to work, volunteer or holiday in these countries, be extra vigilant.

As suggested above, if you've been sexually active while you're away, even if you've used condoms, it's worth having a check up when you return to the UK to make sure you're not infected.

LAWS & CUSTOMS

You might wonder what a country's rule of law has to do with your holiday fling. Well, there are some places in the world where your innocent beach romp could actually see you end up in prison! In some Muslim countries, such as Dubai, having sex outside can lead to a charge of having unmarried sex and public indecency. In countries where Islamic Law is enforced, such as Saudi Arabia, don't partake of any public displays of affection, such as kissing, as it could land you in jail! Check before you travel to a destination (see Chapter 16 for a country information) to find out how liberal the place is.

Also be aware of differences in cultures. You don't want to discover that what you thought was a holiday affair results in you being taken home to meet the parents as a prospective wife/husband. Dating rules are very, very different around the world, like whether it's okay to kiss on a first date. But some things are the same: be sure to tell someone where you're going and with who, make sure they have a contact number and try to avoid being alone with the person until you feel you can trust them and have got to know them a little. Last bit of advice – trust your instincts. If you think the gorgeous surfer guy who's interested is hot and fun, he probably is, so go for it, just don't always expect the relationship to last for the duration of your trip!

Checklist

* Don't get involved with someone if you're
  emotionally vulnerable ☑
* Be wary of con artists ☑
* Don't accept drinks or food from strangers ☑
* Avoid being alone in isolated public places,
  particularly at night ☑
* Keep a note of the Foreign &
  Commonwealth Office contact details ☑
* Carry condoms if you're going to be
  sexually active ☑
* Get a sexual health check before and
  after travel if you're sexually active ☑
* Be extra vigilant in AIDS/HIV hot spots ☑
* Abide by local laws and customs when dating ☑

Chapter 14
Keeping in touch

It has never been easier to keep in touch with home while you're away. Gone are the days of writing a postcard (although that's nice to do from time to time!), now you can be in instant communication with friends and family all over the world.

TELEPHONE

Nothing beats a quick call home every now and again when you're travelling. But before you so much as dial a digit make sure you know what options there are to ensure you don't end up paying the equivalent of half your airfare home for a five-minute chat.

If you take your mobile phone away with you then it can be tempting to use it for chatting and texting much as you would at home. It's really important if you're on a budget that you check with your network provider how much calls and texts will be while you're away as you may get some huge bills if you're not careful.

If you're away for a long period, ask your provider if they have an international traveller package which provides cheaper calls abroad, though be sure to check how long you'd be committed to paying for the service. Make sure your provider sets you up with international roaming, which can take up to a week, so you'll be able to receive and make calls straight away from the moment you touch down.

You'll also need to make sure that your phone will work in the countries that you're travelling to. This information may be supplied on your provider's website, such as T-Mobile, which allows you to click on a world map and match it to your phone model to find out compatibility. Otherwise, call up customer services and get them to check.

A few top phone tips I've been given are to take a small address book, with phone numbers, in your luggage – if all of your emergency contacts are on your mobile phone and it's stolen, how will you get in contact with home? Also, save the numbers of the nearest British Embassy, High Commission or Consulate in the countries that you're visiting to your phone before you travel, plus the numbers of any hotels or guides.

Top Travel Tip

Jot down (in your address book!) the number of your mobile phone provider's customer service number and your phone's serial number, so that if it's stolen you can make sure the phone and SIM card are blocked straight away.

Using pre-paid international call cards is an economical and easy way to keep in touch and to keep a lid on your budget. These cards come in pre-paid denominations (usually £5, £10 or £20) and come equipped with a local number through which you make your long-distance call. It's a good idea to keep a calling card with you at all times in case of an emergency.

Another option, which may not go down so well at the other end, is to reverse charge calls. It's easy, simply phone the operator, give them the number and get them to ask the person you're calling if they will accept the charges. Obviously if you want to maintain good relations back home you should only use this method if you've agreed beforehand that's it's okay, or in emergencies!

ONLINE

If you don't already have one, set up a web-based email. Gmail (www.gmail.com), Yahoo (www.mail.yahoo.com) and Hotmail (www.hotmail.com) are very popular, very easy to set up and can be used from any computer. A great tip is to make sure that you have your friends' and family's email addresses already keyed into your web account to save time; it will come up immediately when you type in their name and is useful if you want to send multiple emails in one go – vital if the clock's ticking in an Internet café!

If you want to keep in touch on the move via email, then consider buying (if you don't already have one) a BlackBerry (http://eu.blackberry.com/eng/). This nifty bit of kit also has a phone, media player, camera and has Bluetooth; some of the newer models also have GPS navigation, perfect for helping you find your way out of the jungle.

Skype (www.skype.com), which allows you to make unlimited free calls from your computer, has been a fantastic development for travellers as it means no more expensive calls home. On the plus side, you can call friends anywhere in the world, video call and instant message for free. The downside is that it's only free to call other Skype users, so if your mum and best mate aren't with Skype, it's going to cost you.

It's really easy to stay in touch online by blogging (keeping a web log). By creating your own website, which you can upload text, pictures and videos to as you go, means your mates can log on whenever they want to see what you're up to. You can build your own if you're computer savvy.

Top Travel Tip

If setting up a web log sounds like rocket science, companies like STA, www.statravel.co.uk, help you set up a simple, personal travel blog that's really easy to update online.

Facebook (www.facebook.com), the social networking site, is a great way of keeping in touch with all your family and friends in one go, provided you get them all to become members, which is a pretty simple process. As well as being able to read about what you've been up to, they'll be able to *see* what you've been up to if you've got a digital camera and upload the images.

If you're a keen photographer and not big on writing, then there are some photo sharing websites that might appeal. Sites such as www.flickr.com allow you to upload your snaps and share them with your friends by sending them a link. You have to sign up to be a member, but it's free and easy to do.

Of course, to keep in touch with home via the web you're going to need a computer, or at least access to one. Some travellers pop their slim laptops into their backpack, seeing it as an essential part of their travel. If you're doing this, make sure it's included in your insurance and don't forget to pack all of the extras, like charger and cables to transfers pictures from your camera to your computer. There's nothing more frustrating than arriving in the middle of nowhere and realising you're missing a vital piece of kit. If you're not taking a computer, you'll be reliant on Internet cafés, which are available all over the world and charge a variety of rates for usage. Take a look at www.cybercafes.com to locate ones in the country you're travelling to; the site even provides opening times, addresses and prices, though these are all subject to change.

Checklist

* Enquire about a traveller package for
  your mobile   ☑
* Take an address book, with emergency as
  well as friends' numbers   ☑
* Save the numbers of British Embassies in
  the countries you're visiting to your mobile   ☑
* Buy a pre-paid international call card for
  emergencies   ☑
* Set up a private online email account if
  you don't already have one   ☑
* Consider taking gadgets, such as a
  BlackBerry or laptop   ☑
* Sign up to Skype for free online phone calls   ☑
* Keep in touch online through social
  networking sites   ☑
* Locate cyber cafes in places you'll be
  travelling to   ☑

Chapter 15
Health and safety

Travelling is, for most people, such an exciting thing, both planning and actually going away, that it's easy to forget the risks that accompany it. The assumption that 'it could never happen to me' is all too common, and lack of preparation and knowledge is one of the key causes of illness or injury when people head off abroad.

That's not to say that you should wrap yourself up in cotton wool and never leave your house, but it's essential that you investigate how you're travelling, where you're travelling to, what dangers there are there and what precautions you need to take before you arrive.

ANIMALS

The most dangerous animal to man isn't a predator like a lion or shark, it's actually the humble mosquito, in particular the female anopheline variety, which is responsible for killing millions of people each year by infecting them with malaria. For information about how to protect yourself from this insect and the disease, turn to page 152 in this chapter. There are hundreds of other animals and insects that pose a threat to humans in varying degrees, but there isn't enough room to cover them all, so I've focused on the most prolific.

Crocodiles are a threat if you're travelling to the tropics.

These large reptiles cause hundreds of deaths a year. You should never enter water which may contain them, which rules out spontaneous bathing in many rivers, lakes and ponds in much of Asia, Africa, the Americas and Australia. You're more at risk in East Africa and Asia in particular as they're home to the most dangerous types, saltwater and Nile crocodiles, which can grow up to 8m (26ft) long. One of the problems, for locals and tourists alike, is that they're hard to spot as they often lie below the water's surface, so what may look like a beautiful, clear pool may in fact contain several crocs just waiting for a meal. They usually attack in the shallows and are incredibly fast, so the victim has little chance of getting away. Don't necessarily think that because locals are washing or fishing by the edge of a river or lake that it is safe, they are often doing this out of necessity and know the risks involved. In the event of a crocodile attack, your only hope is to stab it in the eyes with a knife, or sharp object, or even your fingers.

Elephants, which are herbivores and not readily associated with danger like, say, a lion or shark, actually cause more than 600 deaths per year worldwide, but predominantly in Asia and Africa. Most of these deaths aren't caused by lone bull elephants in the bush, they're actually caused by elephant – human conflict. This basically means that a growth in human population has meant the loss of elephant's habitat due to housing and farming, so the elephants have little choice but to raid crops and villages. In India, deaths caused by elephants are around 200 per year and rising, and the figure is also growing in Africa. So, if you're going to be in an area with elephants, you need to know how to behave. Firstly, if you do encounter elephants when you're out walking, don't run, and quietly move away downwind. Elephants have poor visual perception, but they have keen hearing and a highly developed sense of smell. Mock charges, especially by old and lone bulls, are characterised by the ears spread out and a loud trumpeting, and may end a few metres away, after which the elephant retreats. To run away may be fatal. In case of a real charge, which is characterised by the ears flattened against the body with the trunk curled up, run for your life and remember that climbing the highest tree won't help, as they're able to push down and trample fairly big trees.

Hippopotami are vegetarian and placid when left alone. However, they are considered to be Africa's most-dangerous large game, and are reputed to kill more people every year than predators such as lions or crocodiles, when provoked. It's really important that you try to avoid them, so always travel with a guide if you're in water where hippos live, as they're often hard to spot. Solitary bulls and cows with calves can quickly become aggressive and there are lots of reports of small boats and canoes being overturned and the occupants bitten to death. Hippos demonstrate aggression by opening the mouth, displaying their large teeth and making short charges through the water, so it's best to avoid the edge of rivers if you're not sure what lives there. When a grazing hippo is disturbed, it is dangerous to be between it and the water, as it will blindly run along its well-worn path back to the water, trampling anything in its way. And don't camp at or near hippo paths or waterholes, as they're attracted to fires and lights. Be careful in dry seasons; when hippo are concentrated in small waterholes they feel threatened in the shallow water and may charge random passers by.

Jellyfish encounters are rarely fatal, particularly in Europe, where a swim in the sea may result in a painful sting or two, but nothing life-threatening. However, you do need to be aware that some species of jellyfish, such as the poisonous box jellyfish found in Australia, Hawaii, Vietnam and other tropical countries, can cause death. Despite its tiny size (a thumbnail) its venom is the most deadly in the animal kingdom and it's caused at least 568 recorded deaths since 1954. They're particularly prevalent in the warm waters of northern Australia, but the swarms tend to disappear during the Aussie winter. If you're visiting the country on your travels during the summer months, make sure you swim on beaches that have nets to protect swimmers. If you do get stung by any kind of jellyfish, vinegar, applied for 30 seconds, can help prevent the jellyfish's nematocysts (stinging cells to you and me) discharging into the bloodstream. It can also be used to help remove any tentacles – note, use a towel or gloves for this as tentacles can still sting even when separated from the main body. There are loads of myths about how to stop the stinging, from human urine to alcohol and ammonia, but the experts reckon that some of these may even hasten the venom release.

Top Travel Tip

Be smart and carry a little bottle of vinegar in your rucksack if you're planning on a marine adventure – it has saved dozens of lives of people stung by jellyfish on Australian beaches.

Dogs, foxes and bats may sound like innocent enough animals when compared to crocs, raging hippos and box jellyfish, but they're all potential rabies carriers, so should be treated with caution. Often characterised by unusual behaviour, like wandering around aimlessly with saliva dribbling from its mouth, appearing very tame or aggressive, or showing signs of convulsion or partial paralysis, animals with rabies have been known to attack humans and should be avoided at all costs.

Make sure you have a rabies inoculation before you travel, and don't discount this if you're travelling around Europe as it's still present throughout the continent. It's estimated that there are around 40,000 deaths from rabies worldwide per year, so patting that little puppy lying in the street might not be such a good idea with these statistics in mind. If you're unlucky enough to be bitten by a rabid animal it's vital to get to a hospital as soon as possible and the bite wounds must be washed and disinfected immediately.

Snakes are found in most parts of the world, but only around 15 per cent of the 3,000 or so different types of poisonous snakes that exist are regarded as posing a potential risk to humans. Most of these are to be found in tropical and sub tropical regions, most of the United States (except Alaska, Maine and Hawaii) and Australia. According to an article published in the US Public Library of Science Medicine, around 400,000 people are poisoned worldwide each year, with 20,000 bites resulting in death. India has the highest figures, with 81,000 poisonings, followed by Sri Lanka (33,000), Vietnam (30,000), Brazil (30,000) and Mexico (28,000), but experts predict the real figures are much higher as many victims, particularly in African countries such as Nigeria and Kenya, don't seek hospital treatment.

With this in mind, it's important to avoid snakebites while you're away. Eighty-five per cent of bites occur below the knee, so wear long boots or trousers in snake-prevalent areas. Make a noise (snakes are deaf but respond to vibrations) by stamping your feet and bash the area ahead with a long branch. If you see a snake, stand still, instinctively they'll move away – most snakes aren't overtly aggressive and avoid trouble, apart from the Australian Taipan, which strikes unpredictably, as does the puff adder – and are more likely to attack a moving target. Don't put your hand into holes or cracks in rocks, even if you've dropped something; fetch it out with a stick, not your hand and of course never, ever pick up a snake. If you're in the water you're not free from danger; sea snakes, found in Southeast Asia and Australia, are highly dangerous and snorkellers and divers are advised to keep well away from them.

In the event that you are bitten by a snake, the first thing is not to panic; as mentioned above, only a few snakes are really dangerous to humans, and often no venom is used in the first bite. The second thing is to avoid an unnecessary movement to prevent the venom from spreading quickly around the body, but if possible, wash the site of the bite with clean water and soap. A bandage can be placed firmly over and around the bite to help reduce the venom spreading, but it mustn't be too tight and a pulse must still be felt; airways should be kept free of vomit and blood.

The recovery position should be used if there's prolonged vomiting to stop sick going down into the airways and lungs. Luckily, most snakebites are quite slow acting, from four to 20 hours, so there's usually time to get to a doctor or hospital for anti-venom. First-aid measures that aren't recommended include sucking the venom out and cutting around the bite to stop the venom spreading.

Spiders

Most spider bites are harmless and don't require first aid. However, if you're travelling to Australia or Central and South America, it's worth noting that there are venomous spiders so you need to be aware of the dangers.

In Central and South America there are lots of arachnids, from the world's smallest to the largest. The Brazilian wandering spider is a large, brown spider, which is extremely fast and is regarded as among the most dangerous spiders in the world due to its highly toxic venom. Large New World tarantulas (those indigenous to the Americas) may look scary, but have bites that generally pose little threat to humans other than causing localised pain. The primary means of defense for these spiders are urticating hairs, which can cause irritation.

In Australia it's the funnel-web spider which is most feared. In particular, the Sydney funnel-web spider, a bulky, black spider, found in a relatively small area around the city of Sydney, frequently bites people and is regarded as among the most dangerous in the world. The widow spiders such as the black widow, redback spider and katipo also have a toxic venom and are similar to large house spiders but with a dark shiny abdomen and one or several red spots on its body.

The six-eyed sand spider in southern Africa is another of the world's most venomous spiders. Unfortunately no anti-venom currently exists for its bite; fortunately, it rarely interacts with humans, and is seldom known to bite. Like the recluse spider, this variety buries itself in sand and strikes from its ambush at prey that wanders too closely

In the case of any spider bite that causes discomfort it's important to go to a hospital. It's also a helpful to know the culprit, so rather than squashing the spider, try to capture it and take it so a correct diagnosis can be made. To prevent bites, always check your footwear before putting them on, shake out clothes and be extra careful outside if you're moving leaves, rocks and twigs.

DISEASES

There isn't room to list all of the diseases in the world; in fact there are some tropical diseases that completely baffle doctors so we don't even know all of them. With this in mind, I'm going to outline the major ones, which affect millions of people around the world and which you should get vaccinations for, if possible, before you jet off.

Your first step towards travel health and safety is to find out if you need inoculations, well in advance of your trip; it's really important that you don't leave it until the last minute as some vaccines take time to get into your system and become effective, with some being administered in stages. You should be able to get most jabs from your GP, some are available on the NHS for free, or just the cost of the prescription charge, while others you have to pay for, such as rabies and diptheria. How much your GP charges you seems to be the luck of the draw – I've had the same injections as someone else going on the same trip and paid much more money in London than they did in the Midlands. Alternatively, you can opt to get your vaccinations at a travel clinic; log on to www.travelhealth.co.uk to find your nearest. It can amount to a lot of money, £100 plus, if you're going to get five or six done. Be sure to check whether the price includes one shot or a complete dose if you need a vaccine that requires several doses, like hepatitis B.

You'll need to be able to provide your GP with some important information before they're able to decide exactly what vaccinations you need. These include which countries you're visiting and how long for; what sort of places you'll be travelling to, such as remote rural areas or mainly cities; where you'll be staying, such as camping or up-market hotels; whether you have any allergies or illnesses; if you're pregnant or likely to become so and if you're on any medication.

Once you've had your inoculations, be sure to keep a record of them. Your GP or travel clinic should give you a small booklet with details of which jabs you've had and the dates they were administered – if they don't provide one, ask for one as they can be vital. For example, some countries won't allow you to enter if you haven't had a yellow fever inoculation and you're entering from a country where it's rife.

While you're travelling, be aware that some diseases are

water- or food-borne so it's really important to stay vigilant and not to get complacent if you've been in a destination for a few months. As a rule with food – boil it, cook it, peel it or leave it!

Top Travel Tip

Keep your health booklet in your passport so it's easy for officials to see that you're fully inoculated.

Bilharzia

A water-borne disease that affects around 200 million people in 74 countries across the tropics. It's caused by a parasitic worm commonly found in shallow water that is stagnant or flowing slowly, like banks of rivers or pools, especially where plants are growing in the water.

Symptoms: When the skin is penetrated, the first symptom may be a skin reaction, although this may be mild or not even show. Other symptoms include persistent fatigue, bodily discomfort, fever and vague intestinal complaints. Bilharzia infection can be severely debilitating and unpleasant and is not easily cured. In rare cases it can spread to the brain, with lethal results. There isn't a vaccine and if in doubt, a doctor should be consulted.

How to avoid: Ask locals about areas known to have bilharzia and avoid them. If you come into contact with contaminated water, clean yourself immediately by rigorously rubbing yourself dry with a cloth, as the parasite can penetrate the skin within minutes. Water should be boiled or purified before being used for drinking or washing.

Most common: All over Africa; parts of the Middle East; South America; Southeast Asia.

Dengue fever

There are around 50 million cases of dengue fever each year all over the world, including Australia, southern United States, Africa, South America, the Far East and Middle East. The Aedes mosquito, which has a black and white body, spreads it and you can't catch it from another person.

Symptoms: Very similar to malaria – high fever, lethargy, headache and joint pains. Signs appear about five to eight days after you've been bitten and diarrhoea and a rash are also common. It's usual to have it for up to 10 days, after which you may suffer from acute fatigue and depression for several weeks.

How to avoid: It's a really debilitating disease to get while you're travelling, so try to avoid getting mosquito bites. Cover up in the mornings and evenings, use insect repellent and mosquito nets at night.

Most common: Throughout the tropics; sub-Saharan Africa, Asia, Caribbean, Central and South America.

Hepatitis

The Latin word for liver inflammation, which is exactly what this nasty disease is, but it can also lead to destruction of liver cells as well as being inflammatory. There are various types.

Type A

It can be transmitted directly from contaminated food, like shellfish, or by a food handler with hepatitis A, as well as contaminated water and other beverages. The virus can also be spread through contact with an infected person's stools through poor hygiene.

Symptoms: First symptoms include loss of appetite, nausea, aching muscles and joints and a mild fever. Later symptoms include yellowing of the skin, mucous membranes, light-coloured stools and dark urine.

How to avoid: A vaccine for Type A hepatitis is available. You'll receive two injections, six to 12 months apart. It has a protection rate of 95 per cent and lasts for at least 10 years. The vaccine is recommended if you're taking trips to countries where the general standard of hygiene is very poor, such as Asian, South American and African countries. But the way to avoid it is to wash your hands and exercise extreme caution with food and water in endemic areas.

Most common: Worldwide, excluding North America, Europe, Australia and New Zealand.

Type B

Can be spread in a number of ways; by contact with blood from an infected person, such as blood transfusion or contaminated needles used by drug addicts, tattooists or acupuncturists. It can also be spread by sexual contact with an infected person. (See sexually transmitted diseases in Chapter 13).

Symptoms: Fever, fatigue, muscle or joint pain, loss of appetite, severe nausea and vomiting, yellow eyes and skin and bulging stomach.

How to avoid: There is a vaccine for Type B, but to prevent yourself from exposure to the disease, practise safe sex, avoid contact with blood and bodily fluids, avoid sharing sharp items such as razors, needles, nail clippers, toothbrushes, and earrings or body rings.

Most common: Asia, South America, Africa and Eastern Europe.

Type C

It's estimated there are more than 170 million carriers and it is hard to treat. It can be transmitted through contact with an infected person's blood, through sexual contact (though the risk is very small) and by using a contaminated needle.

Symptoms: Poor appetite, lack of interest in food, nausea, aching muscles and joints and light fever. Later symptoms include yellowing of skin, mucous membranes, light-coloured stools and dark urine.

How to avoid: There isn't currently a vaccine for hepatitis C.

Most common: Asia, South America, Africa and Eastern Europe.

HIV/AIDS (See Chapter 13)

Tetanus

This is caused by bacteria spores, which can be found in soil, dust and manure all over the world. It enters the human body through punctured skin, such as a pinprick, scratch or wound.

Symptoms: Headache, fever, restlessness, irritability and jaw muscles spasms spreading to the face, neck, limbs and torso. It's a dangerous, potentially fatal, disease, which can lead to blood clots on lungs, pneumonia and coma.

How to avoid: Thorough cleaning will help prevent infection, covering wounds and getting an up-to-date vaccination. Most people in the UK have been vaccinated during childhood, but it's a good idea to have a booster from your doctor every 10 years, particularly if you're travelling.

Most common: Particularly prevalent in Southeast Asia, India, some parts of Africa and South America.

Typhoid fever

The disease is transmitted from human to human via contaminated food or drinking water, so unhygienic and unsanitary conditions are the main cause of infection. It's found in large parts of Asia, Africa, Central and South America, where it occasionally causes epidemics. The World Health

Organisation (WHO) estimates that there are approximately 16 million cases a year, which result in 600,000 deaths.

Symptoms: An infectious, feverish disease with severe symptoms in the digestive system in the second phase of the illness. Classic typhoid fever is a serious disease. It can be life threatening, but antibiotics are an effective treatment.

How to avoid: The disease lasts several weeks and convalescence takes some time. There are several forms of vaccine to protect you. Most travel clinics use the injectable form (Typherix or Typhim Vi) rather than the oral form (Vivotif). The injectable vaccine is easier to administer since it only requires one dose and has fewer side effects. It should be administered at least two weeks prior to potential typhoid exposure and is effective for three years.

Most common: Africa, Asia, Central and South America.

Yellow fever

A very serious viral infection transmitted by mosquitoes. The virus is permanently prevalent, with a more or less constant number of sufferers in several tropical regions of Africa and on the continent of America. Yellow fever has sudden epidemics, with a mortality rate of almost 50 per cent. The virus is transmitted among humans by a couple of species of mosquito, including Aedes aegyptii, which can also transmit dengue fever. Every year about 200,000 cases of yellow fever are recorded, and 30,000 of these are fatal, but it is thought that the figures are considerably higher in reality.

Symptoms: In mild cases the symptoms are similar to flu, but serious cases develop a high temperature and may have a series of after effects, such as internal bleeding, kidney failure and meningitis. A classic feature of yellow fever is hepatitis, which is the reason for the yellow colouring of the skin (jaundice) and the name of the disease.

How to avoid: There is a vaccine, which is very effective against yellow fever. It protects you from 10 days after the vaccination, which is administered in a single injection. Current advice is to have it repeated every 10 years. In some countries where there are mosquitoes that could transmit the virus, actual documentation is required, stating that you have been vaccinated against yellow fever before you can obtain permission to enter the country. This can be provided by a stamp in the yellow international vaccination card issued by the WHO (www.who.int), which your GP will give to you.

Most common: Endemic in Africa and Latin American countries.

Malaria

The statistics for malaria are pretty shocking; around 515 million cases per year resulting in one to three million deaths. Most cases occur in sub-Saharan Africa, but it's widespread in tropical and sub-tropical regions, including most of the Americas, Asia and Africa.

A malaria-carrying mosquito takes blood from an infected person, around a week later it bites someone else and the infected blood gets mixed with the fresh blood when the mosquito's saliva is injected into the person being bitten. The parasites quickly multiply in red blood cells and can cause symptoms including light headedness, shortness of breath, fever, chills and nausea. In severe cases the person infected slips into a coma and may even die depending on the strain.

At present there isn't a cure for malaria, however, there are preventative drugs that you can take to reduce infection. While it's possible to build up a resistance to the disease, if you're not from an endemic area, you're at high risk and it's therefore essential to take precautions.

When I was updating my jabs recently for a trip to Zambia,

a doctor told me that the best way to fight malaria is not to get bitten in the first place, which is sound advice. In light of this, pack a mosquito net. They're very light and vital if you're staying in budget accommodation, or sleeping outdoors, in a country that has malaria.

Secondly, take plenty of insect repellent. There are some fantastic sprays and creams on the market; look for ones with DEET. Jungle Formula (www.jungleformula.co.uk), which is approved by the Hospital for Tropical Diseases, is good at keeping bugs at bay, but you need to keep applying it regularly. You could also invest in a range of clothing infused with permethrin to repel mosquitoes, which you can pick up in outdoors shops. At night, when you're most at risk of being bitten, cover up; this means long sleeves, trousers and shawls, basically, the smaller the amount of flesh exposed the smaller the risk.

If you're definitely visiting a high-risk area then it's advisable to visit your doctor and take a course of anti-malarial tablets.

Top Travel Tip

Don't believe seasoned travellers that tell you a gin & tonic will keep mosquitoes at bay, that myth stems from a time when colonialists used gin to take a dose of quinine, believed to help fight malaria.

Malaria tablets

Some people are put off the idea of medication because it can cost quite a lot of money and because of the side effects, but, as you've just read, the number of deaths per year is too high to risk it.

Malarone tablets contain two active ingredients, proguanil hydrochloride and atovaquone, both medicines that are active against the parasite that causes malaria by stopping the parasite from reproducing once it is in the bloodstream. To prevent malaria, Malarone has to be taken once a day and you need to start taking it 24 to 48 hours before entering the malarial area. It should then be taken during the stay (which should not exceed 28 days) and be continued for seven days after leaving the area.

Lariam is another option offered by GPs. It contains the active ingredient mefloquine, which is a type of medicine called an antimalarial, used in both the prevention and treatment of malaria. Mefloquine works by attacking the parasites once they have entered the red blood cells, stopping them from multiplying further. The course of tablets should be started at least one week but preferably two to three weeks before travel to the malaria region, and should be taken throughout your stay so that if you are bitten by an infected mosquito, there will be medicine in your blood to prevent malaria developing. You should continue to take tablets for a further four weeks after leaving the malaria area to kill any remaining parasites released from the liver into the red blood cells during this time.

The down side of Lariam is that it has been connected in some people to psychiatric side effects such as mood or behaviour changes, anxiety, depression, feelings of persecution, crying, aggression, forgetfulness, agitation, confusion or hallucinations. If affected you should stop taking this medicine and consult a doctor immediately. In 75 per cent of cases such side effects appear by the third dose if they are going to affect you. For this reason, if taking mefloquine to prevent malaria it is recommended you start taking it three weeks before travel, so that if affected you can be prescribed an alternative preventative medicine.

To find out more about your options, have a look at

www.netdoctor.co.uk, which will give you the lowdown on malaria and prevention.

ENVIRONMENT

Insect-borne diseases, animal attacks or illness caused by food are some of the obvious concerns running through a traveller's mind before embarking on an adventure, but in actual fact it's often the environment that you're entering, rather than what lives or is served up there, which can be detrimental to your health.

Snow & cold

Few things are more miserable than your body being exposed to extremely low temperatures when you're not adequately prepared. If any part of your trip is going to involve snow, ice or below-average temperatures and high winds, then it's essential that you pack accordingly, unless you want to be at best uncomfortable, or at worst put your health at great risk.

You're going to need to invest in decent clothing which can withstand plummeting temperatures and extreme conditions. I'd recommend a Gore-Tex garment which is waterproof and wind resistant but breathable, and all the necessary accessories including gloves, hat, scarf and quality footwear which isn't going to let in water and has excellent grip. Bypass fashion stores for all of these items and head straight for your nearest mountaineering or adventure sports shop to ensure you get a high standard, it's not something you can afford to skimp on.

If you're travelling on mountains, exposed hillsides or deserts (they may be scorching in the day, but temperatures can drop below freezing at night), it's essential that you take precautions. Always travel with at least one other person; it's very dangerous to be in mountainous areas alone as there's no one else to summon help should you get into difficulties. Make sure that someone knows where you're planning to travel to and roughly how long that should take. Have all the necessary equipment other than clothing, such as maps, compass and supplies, including water and packed food, and plenty of plastic bags to keep everything dry.

Don't forget to cover your extremities like fingers, and wear multiple layers of clothing, as this is better for trapping heat rather than one big layer. Always wear a hat in the cold (body heat is lost from the top of the head), try to keep dry as much as possible, keep active so your circulation is working (which produces heat) and eat plenty of carbohydrates as they're a great energy source for your body.

Top Travel Tip

Make sure you layer up if you're travelling in extreme conditions. Layers trap heat and will help to keep your body warm; and don't forget a hat as you lose heat from the top of your head as well as other exposed parts, like hands.

If you're well prepared, then you really have lessened the chance of anything bad occurring while you're actually on your holiday. However, there are still things to watch out for. Frostbite, which occurs when skin left unprotected freezes rupturing cells and damaging tissue, can vary from superficial harm to permanent damage that can result in gangrene and possibly amputation depending on the length of exposure. While any bit of your body can be affected, it's the extremities, like fingers, ears and toes that are especially vulnerable, so it's essential that you have decent protection for these and keep them covered at all times when you're out in severe weather conditions, like blizzards or high wind chill.

Frostbite can happen very quickly, within minutes, if the temperature is below zero and you're not dressed suitably. An early symptom is a tingling sensation, which can lead to the area turning numb and white. People are often unaware of the problem at first, so it's really important that you look out for early signs so that you can take steps to treat the frostbite before it gets more severe, particularly if medical help isn't readily available. If the skin of the affected area is still soft to touch, but showing signs of frostbite, start moving to get the circulation going, also try massaging the area and if it's exposed to wet clothing, remove if possible.

Another risk in cold temperatures is hypothermia, which occurs when the body's temperature falls below critical level, generally accepted as 35°C (95°F) by medics. It's foolish to think that hypothermia is something that only happens to extreme mountaineers or off-piste skiers. It's one of the greatest threats to anyone doing an outside sport, so if you're going to be doing something that involves outdoor activities, from walking to sailing, it's vital that you're aware of the risks and know how to tackle them.

As with frostbite, exposure to excessive cold weather is a cause, but so is getting wet in cool conditions (water takes heat away from the body 25 times quicker than air), exhaustion and fatigue, dehydration (fluid loss and heat loss are interconnected) and lack of food. You might also be surprised (and possibly disappointed) to learn that although we assume that a tot of brandy will help warm us up, alcohol in fact dilates the blood vessels to the skin which causes your body to lose heat. Nicotine, found in cigarettes, causes blood vessels to contract and impairs blood flow to the extremities, so, having a drink and a cigarette, if you're in a tricky situation, may make you feel better but isn't going to help matters in the long run.

The early signs of hypothermia are involuntary shivering and feelings of intense cold, particularly in the hands and feet as blood vessels shut down; severe hypothermia causes the muscles to go rigid and the sufferer loses consciousness. This all sounds pretty scary, but the key to preventing hypothermia is very simple; wearing suitable clothes and equipment for the activities you'll be doing.

Sun & heat

You might have your heart set on coming back from a trip as a bronzed beauty, but being out and about without adequate protection in sunshine that's much stronger than you're used to isn't wise. Extreme sun exposure can be very dangerous. The immediate effects are harming; itchy or burnt skin which goes red and may blister before peeling, and can be very painful. And the long-term effects even more so; sun exposure is linked to a rise in the number of skin cancer diagnoses each year in the UK, plus it also leads to premature aging.

So, while it's tempting to look and feel better now by cultivating a deep tan, it's not worth the risk. Of course it's unrealistic to expect travellers to keep out of the sun between 10am and 3pm daily as experts advise, as even if you're not the sunbathing type, it's likely that you'll be exposed to the sun during activities like snorkelling or trekking.

The answer is to make sure you wear plenty of sunscreen and cover up; wear a hat to protect the top of your head, long sleeved cotton t-shirt to shield your arms and back, and cotton trousers or long-length skirt. Your sun cream should contain Ultraviolet (UV) A and B protection (UVB causes burning, UVA causes deeper, longer term damage), be water resistant and have a sun protection factor (SPF) of at least 25. Sun cream can be expensive but it's vital that you don't scrimp on coverage; you should be getting through a bottle of average-sized lotion or spray per week if you're in the sun every day. And don't forget to cover everywhere, including back of the neck, tops of the ears and your armpits, which are all common places where people get burnt. I religiously cover myself from head to toe in a high-factor sun cream before I even step out of the door when I'm away in a hot country.

Top Travel Tip

You're far more likely to get burnt if you apply sunscreen while you're out and about, as you're bound to be less thorough, so my tip is to apply a thick layer after you've showered, then you have a good base coat for the day and can reapply to certain areas as necessary.

The top of your head is especially vulnerable so you may want to consider investing in a high SPF screen for your hair, available at most hair salons and chemists or, for a simpler option, wear a hat. Your eyes are also vulnerable to sunshine. UV rays can cause cataracts or even melanoma at the back of the eye, so buy some decent sunglasses (cheap ones rarely properly block out UV rays) and wear a wide brimmed hat to reduce the amount of sunshine reaching your face. Lips can become sore and cracked if they dry out from sun exposure, so pop a lip balm in your rucksack, preferably with zinc oxide which is great for protecting sun-sensitive areas.

If you do get sunburnt, unfortunately nothing can get rid of it but time. However, there are some things you can do to ease the pain. For a start, stay out of the sun! I'm always amazed when travelling at the amount of people I see with burnt skin who continue to expose themselves. If you have light sunburns, then applying cooling gels, after sun lotions or natural solutions such as aloe vera, will help to ease itching and inflammation. If it's painful, Ibuprofen can help. In the case of severe sunburn, such as blistering over a large area, it's wise to seek medical help.

Heatstroke, which can be caused by many factors such as too much physical exertion, high outside temperatures or sun exposure, occurs when the body is unable to control its temperature due to excessive heat. If you do become a victim of heatstroke, or someone you are travelling with does, then there some immediate things that will ease the situation, such as sitting close to ventilation, like a fan or open window, sipping water, showering the skin with cool (but not cold) water, covering the body in damp towels or sheets and massaging the skin to encourage circulation. In severe heatstroke cases, such as vomiting or unconsciousness, it's vital to get professional medical help as quickly as possible so that oxygen and intravenous fluids through a drip can be used to regulate the body's temperature.

FLYING

Airports can be very busy, stressful places. To avoid unnecessary panicking always try and arrive for your flight early and, if possible, check-in online as this saves lots of time and unnecessary queuing.

It's not just the stress of the airport that can have an adverse affect on your body, it's also flying itself. It can be extremely harmful to fly if you have certain medical conditions, so it's essential that you consult your GP before you head off on holiday if you're at all worried.

Possibly the most well-known side effect is DVT (deep vein thrombosis), which has hit the headlines several times after people have flown long-haul and developed a clot. Doctors advise wearing flight socks, which you can pick up at most airports, and moving around the cabin regularly as ways to avoid DVT, particularly lengthy flights.

There are certain conditions which mean you shouldn't fly. These include suspected collapsed lung; chest surgery within the previous four weeks; two days after breaking a bone; more than 36 weeks pregnant (some airlines request a certificate from your doctor specifying the predicted due date); scuba diving (depends how deep you've gone, but usually don't dive the day before a flight) and you shouldn't fly after eye surgery, until a specialist gives you the all clear to do so.

There are other circumstances when it's okay to fly, but only if you have taken the necessary precautions. These include asthma – make sure your symptoms are under control before boarding and carry your inhaler; if you have a severe respiratory condition, like emphysema, the airline may allow you to use supplemental oxygen.

Fear of flying

Many people don't like flying, but for some it's a phobia (aerophobia) and means they can't even board an aircraft. If this is the case, it really might be time to book yourself on a course aimed at combating flying phobia. Virgin Airlines runs a Flying Without Fear programme (www.flyingwithoutfear. info), which includes explaining what all the noises on planes are (i.e. when the wheels come down for landing, it's not a wing falling off!), why turbulence is safe and the science of flight. It claims to have a 98 per cent success rate, although at £199 it's pricey.

Other things to consider include hypnosis and learning relaxation techniques. Medication, such as diazepam, which sedates, is something that has to be discussed with your doctor. There are certain things you can do to help yourself, such as letting flight crew know you're a nervous flier when you board, putting drops of lavender oil on your pillow (it's calming), taking camomile teabags on board (also calming) and Bach Rescue Remedy, either cream or drops.

Top Travel Tip

A couple of lavender drops on your flight pillow will help to induce sleep and calm the nerves.

FOOD & DRINK

This section may seem like teaching your grandmother to suck eggs (sucking eggs would be inadvisable by the way as there's a low risk of salmonella!), but thousands of people fall ill on trips every year because they haven't been careful when it comes to eating and drinking. Following a few simple suggestions could mean the difference between having a healthy holiday and being laid up ill in bed for days, or worse, weeks.

When you're away, you're going to be exposed to all sorts of exciting foods, from street stalls to dinner in a local's home. Naturally, it's desirable to try out cuisine from the country you're visiting, finding new foods is one of the many wonderful things about travelling. However, bear in mind the following before you consume everything you find on your plate or in your glass.

Firstly, it depends where you're travelling. If your adventure takes you to developing countries, the reality is that there will be a higher risk of infection from water- or food-borne illnesses, such as typhoid, hepatitis A or diarrhoea.

Be wary of any food that isn't fresh. If meat or fish has been outside on a street stall, uncovered, not only is it at risk of being contaminated by flies, you also have no idea how long it has been there, so there's a serious risk of contamination. Unless something is cooked in front of you, don't go there.

What's on offer may not be conventional meat that you're used to, with goat, dog or horse sometimes substituted for sheep or pig, or guinea pig in places like Peru. Whatever the meat on offer, make sure it's always cooked well, as there's less chance of contamination.

Chances are you're going to be dining out on seafood if you're by the coast. If that's the case, the fresher the better, preferably caught that morning. In a hot country, fish can go off very quickly, so if you're eating it in a city far from the sea, think twice. Shellfish carry the most risk as they filter water, which can often be polluted.

Rice, the staple diet of many developing countries, may look innocuous, but it can actually contain bacteria that multiply quickly when the rice cools, causing severe sickness and diarrhoea. If you're travelling to a country where other forms of food aren't readily available, and there aren't many other options but rice, then it's really important that you find out when it was cooked, preferably seeing it made. With this in mind, avoid street stalls that don't prepare food before your eyes and where the dishes might have been hanging around for days.

Water is something to watch out for. If possible, drink bottled water; always making sure the cap seal is in place. If bottled water isn't possible, drink water that has boiled for at least one minute and if that's not possible, then you can rely on iodine, which is a chemical purifier that you can easily pick up at camping stores or chemists. Don't forget that water isn't just about what you drink; it's also about what you eat. Salad will have been washed in water, which may be contaminated, ditto fruit unless you've been able to peel it.

Ice cubes are likely to have been made from the water you're trying to avoid, so don't have drinks on the rocks, and cleaning your teeth in non-treated water can put you at risk of water-borne infections.

Checklist

* Know your enemy when it comes to
  dangerous animals ☑
* Check which inoculations you need
  well before departure ☑
* Get travel vaccinations from a GP or
  travel clinic ☑
* Get a health passport ☑
* Buy malaria tablets if necessary for
  your destinations ☑
* Stock up on appropriate clothing/
  essentials for sun/snow ☑
* Avoid DVT on long-haul flights by moving
  around regularly and wearing flight socks ☑
* Avoid contaminated water and food ☑

Chapter 16
Country guide A–Z

The following country-by-country guide also includes a section on safety. This isn't meant to put you off, but it's really important to know about the major risks of anywhere that you're travelling to. Advice from the FCO is correct at the time of publication, but please check regularly for updates.

For entry requirements, this is for those that hold valid British passports.

AFRICA

Benin

Climate: Very hot, particularly in the north which is dry and arid.

Safety: Crime is a problem, especially highway banditry and vehicle jackings. Medical facilities are poor, particularly in rural areas. Waterborne disease such as cholera and malaria are common. Only use boiled or bottled water.

Entry: A visa is needed before entering the country. If you want to travel to neighbouring Nigeria or Ghana, you'll need to arrange separate visas prior to travelling as they're not available in Benin. There's no UK embassy in Benin or Benin embassy in the UK; in emergencies contact the British embassy in neighbouring Nigeria.

Contact: Benin Consulate, 020 8830 8612.

Botswana

Climate: Very hot. Ranges from semi-arid to sub-tropical and gets humid in the rainy season (November to April).

Safety: Crime against tourists is rare, but there is some petty crime in larger towns like Gaborone. Malaria risk so take precautions.

Entry: No visas and you can stay for up to 90 days.

Contact: http://ukinbotswana.fco.gov.uk

Burkina Faso

Climate: This tiny state is sub-Saharan. Most of the country is semi-desert and is constantly hot and dry.

Safety: High levels of street crime. The FCO advises against travel at night because of the risk of bandits, and scam artists are increasingly targeting foreign visitors. Malaria and waterborne diseases are widespread and medical facilities are limited so take precautions.

Entry: Visa required plus a certificate of vaccination against yellow fever.

Contact: There is no UK embassy, in case of emergencies contact the neighbouring embassy in Ghana. www.britishhighcommission.gov.uk/Ghana

Cameroon

Climate: A mixture of hot desert plains and savannah in the north and tropical rainforest in the south.

Safety: Crime is high and often violent. Armed vehicle jacking and petty theft is rife throughout the country so you need to be vigilant at all times. Rioting and demonstrations are fairly common. Malaria and cholera are widespread and medical facilities poor.

Entry: Visa required and yellow fever vaccination certificate. You also have to register with the British High Commission on arrival in Yaoundé.

Contact: http://ukincameroon.fco.gov.uk

Cape Verde Islands

Climate: Very hot and dry; the islands occasionally suffer from droughts.

Safety: Low crime rates. Serious illness or injury would need air evacuation so make sure you're properly insured.

Entry: No visa needed.

Contact: There's no UK embassy on the island or in the UK, so contact has to be made through the Cape Verde Embassy in Brussels.

Comoros

Climate: This little-known island group off the Mozambique coast has a tropical climate. Hot rainy season runs from November to April, when cyclones can be a problem.

Safety: Crime is rare. Malaria is common and there's an active volcano.

Entry: Visa needed, but available on arrival at Hahaya Airport.

Contact: No official diplomatic contact with the UK either way. Instead, contact the British High Commission in Port Louis, Mauritius to register before travelling to Comoros. http://ukinmauritius.fco.gov.uk

Congo

Climate: This vast central African country has a hot, humid, tropical climate, and most of the country is covered by rainforest.

Safety: The FCO advises against travelling to some areas of the country, particularly the Pool Region where there is sporadic rebel fighting. Crime levels are fairly high and it's not advisable to travel after dark. Health risks include malaria, cholera and Ebola fever. Medical facilities are poor and limited.

Entry: Visa required and a yellow fever vaccination certificate.

Contact: There is no UK representation in the Congo.

Djibouti

Climate: Hot and dry year-round. Coolest months from October to April when there is a little rain.

Safety: The FCO advises against travel to the border region with Eritrea as there are occasional outbreaks of fighting. There's also a risk of banditry away from the capital city. Cholera is common. Credit cards aren't widely used, so visitors need an adequate supply of cash.

Entry: Visa needed. Tourist visas are available for one month, and you can get them when you arrive at the airport or beforehand from the French embassy in London.

Contact: www.ambafrance-uk.org

Egypt

Climate: Hot summers (June to September) and mild winters. In the south it's hot year-round but cooler at night. Little rain apart from the coastal region.

Safety: Terrorist threat; tourists have been targeted and killed in the past. However, armed security does protect most of the key tourist sites and more than a million Brits visited the country in 2007.

Entry: A visa is usually required, although some holiday destinations such as Sharm El Sheikh are exempt for up to 14 days provided you have a valid UK passport.

Contact: www.egyptianconsulat.co.uk

Equatorial Guinea

Climate: Tropical; heavy annual rainfall on the coast, particularly in July and August. Hot Sahara winds blow in the dry season.

Safety: Low crime rate compared to other countries in the region. Foreigners have been targeted for petty theft, so avoid carrying valuables if possible. Malaria, cholera and waterborne diseases are common.

Entry: Visa needed. Yellow fever vaccination certificate required.

Contact: www.embarege-londres.org

Eritrea

Climate: Hot, dry climate with much of the country arid, desert terrain. Subject to droughts.

Safety: The FCO advises against travel in the border areas with Ethiopia, where the political situation is very tense.

Entry: Visa needed and yellow fever vaccination certificate. There are no ATMs in Eritrea, so you'll need cash as credit cards are only accepted in major hotels in capital Asmara.

Contact: www.eritrean-embassy.org.uk

Ethiopia

Climate: East is hot and dry with very serious droughts. Highlands are warm and get some rain in summer (June to September).

Safety: Tense political situation. The FCO advises against travel in the border regions with Eritrea and Somalia. High risk of terrorist attacks. Crime rates are surprisingly low. Malaria and waterborne diseases common throughout.

Entry: Visa needed, which you can get at Addis Ababa Airport on arrival.

Contact: www.ethioembassy.org.uk

Gabon

Climate: Hot, humid year-round; as you'd expect in a country where 85 per cent is tropical rainforest, there's rainfall all year.

Safety: Fairly low crime rates despite much poverty. Malaria and dengue fever occasionally occur.

Entry: Visa required and yellow fever vaccination certificate.

Contact: www.gabonembassy.org

Gambia

Climate: Hot and tropical, with temperatures hovering around 30 degrees. Wettest months between July and September, with very high humidity.

Safety: Crime against tourists has increased so you should remain vigilant. The FCO highlights a risk of visiting very isolated beaches. Travel to areas around the southern border with Senegal should be avoided. Malaria is common, particularly during the rainy season.

Entry: Valid UK passport allows you a 28-day stay. Permission has to be obtained for a longer stay. Yellow fever vaccination certificate may be required if you're travelling from other African countries.

Contact: www.gambia.embassyhomepage.com

Ghana

Climate: Tropical with warm temperatures year-round. North and coastal regions drier than rainforest areas.

Safety: Low terrorism threat. Localised outbreaks of civil unrest; you should avoid political rallies and demonstrations. Crime levels relatively low. Avoid carrying large sums of money or valuables and be very vigilant when drawing cash from ATMs in central Accra. Avoid travelling alone in taxis after dark due to attempted robberies. HIV and AIDS is prevalent, as are malaria and waterborne diseases.

Entry: Visa needed before travel.

Contact: www.ghanahighcommissionuk.com

Guinea-Bissau

Climate: Tropical; rainy season May to November. Humid year-round; coast wetter than the interior.

Safety: Low crime rates, but the country is very poor and in severe economic crisis so take precautions to protect your valuables. If you're travelling to the country by road, avoid the Casamance region where banditry and fighting between separatist groups has occurred.

Entry: Visa needed before travel. The UK doesn't have a Guinea-Bissau embassy, but there is one in Paris.

Contact: Guinea-Bissau Embassy Paris, 0033 9452 61851

Kenya

Climate: Hot, humid and tropical year-round on the coast. Central plateau is temperate. North of the equator, much of the land is arid, semi-desert. Generally, two rainy seasons, March to May and October to December.

Safety: Moderate crime risk, particularly in urban areas such as Nairobi. Malaria risk throughout.

Entry: Visa needed.

Contact: www.kenyahighcommission.net

Lesotho

Climate: Temperate; hot and wet summers and cold winters with snow in the mountains. Rainy season runs October to April.

Safety: Incidences of mugging, vehicle jackings and gun-related robbery in Maseru, which you should avoid walking around after dark. Very high HIV/AIDS rate, so take precautions to avoid exposure.

Entry: Visa needed, can obtain on arrival.

Contact: www.lesotholondon.org.uk

Libya

Climate: Hot and dry year-round, winters are mild and damp. The coast is more temperate but still very hot.

Safety: Instability in the region; don't travel to areas bordering Sudan, Chad, Niger and Algeria. With the exception of border crossings to Tunisia and Egypt, visitors aren't allowed to travel in the interior or border areas without an official guide or permission from the Libyan authorities. Avoid political demonstrations. Low crime rates.

Entry: A visa is required; the Libyan Government is introducing a new visa system requiring applicants to
submit their biometric details, effective from 1
December 2008. You have to visit the Libyan People's
Bureau to give fingerprints and submit the required
documents and passport photos. On 11 November
2007, the Libyan authorities re-imposed a requirement
for all travellers entering the country to have an Arabic
transcript of their passport's details page. If you travel
without this transcript, you may not be able to enter the
country.

Contact: http://libya.embassyhomepage.com

Madagascar

Climate: Tropical; hot and humid. Rainy season from October
to April, but varies according to latitude. Cyclone
season in the east and north from February to March.

Safety: Fairly low crime rate against tourists, but muggings and
robberies do occur so keep valuables out of sight. The
FCO recommends avoiding travelling outside urban
areas as night as there are occasional armed robberies
on the highways. Pickpockets operate in crowded
areas such as airports and markets. Bilharzia, tuber-
culosis, rabies, bubonic plague and malaria are
common to Madagascar. There have also been
reported cases of dengue fever and Chikungunya virus.

Entry: Visa required; can be obtained on arrival.

Contact: www.embassy-madagascar-uk.com

Malawi

Climate: Sub-tropical; hot and humid in the south, cooler in the
highlands. The dry season runs from May to October,
rains from October to April.

Safety: Moderate crime rates involving visitors; majority of
thefts take place around the main bus stations in

Lilongwe and Blantyre and at the port for the Ilala ferry. Armed robbery and carjackings occur. Malaria and rabies are common. Bilharzia can be contracted in many lakeshore areas and rivers. Kasungu National Park is home to tsetse flies carrying sleeping sickness.

Entry: No visa needed.

Contact: www.malawihighcom.org.uk

Mali

Climate: Hot year-round; virtually no rain in the north, rain falls in the south from June to September. Region has droughts and dry desert winds.

Safety: The FCO advises against all travel to the following areas because of fighting between the army and rebel groups, and an increased risk of banditry and kidnap: north and east of the Niger River, apart from to the cities of Timbuktu and Gao; north and west of Timbuktu; and towards the western border with Mauritania. Crime rates in the rest of Mali relatively low. Cholera, malaria and other tropical diseases are common to Mali. Outbreaks of meningitis also occur.

Entry: Visa needed; yellow fever vaccination certificate required.

Contact: No embassy in the UK; contact the Mali British Embassy Liaison Office, 00 223 2021 3412.

Mauritius

Climate: This Indian Ocean island is tropical; hot, sunny days and warm nights. Wetter in December to April, but rain falls year-round.

Safety: Low crime levels but petty theft is increasing.

Entry: No visa needed; if you're arriving from an area where yellow fever exists you'll need a yellow fever vaccination certificate.

Contact: http://Mauritius.embassyhomepage.com

Morocco

Climate: Varied. Coastal areas are Mediterranean; hot summers, mild winters. Central region very hot and arid year-round. Mountains are hot in the summer and very cold in winter, with snow. Sahara desert tops temperatures of 50 degrees in summer, but sometimes very cold nights. Little rainfall.

Safety: Terrorism threat; particularly Casablanca. Violent crime not a major problem, but petty crime on the increase. Credit card fraud and shopping scams common.

Entry: No visa needed. The border between Algeria and Morocco is closed, and no attempt should be made to cross it at any point.

Contact: http://morocco.embassyhomepage.com

Mozambique

Climate: Tropical; hot and humid. Wet season, October to March, dry season April to September.

Safety: Relatively low crime. Robbery occurs in Maputo; avoid using ATM machines on street. Waterborne diseases common throughout.

Entry: Visa needed; can be purchased on arrival, valid for 30 days. Yellow fever vaccination certificate required if you've travelled from a country where the disease exists.

Contact: www.mozambiquehc.org.uk

Namibia

Climate: Hot and sunny year-round. Temperatures can get very hot between December and March. Two rainy seasons, October to December and January to March.

Safety: Beware of pickpockets in town centres, and don't enter townships alone at night, unless you're with someone with local knowledge. Rabies, malaria and cholera are common.

Entry: No visa needed for stays of up to 90 days.

Contact: http://namibia.embassyhomepage.com

Niger

Climate: Hot year-round. Very dry country; south gets some rain in May. Coolest months May to September.

Safety: High risk if travelling outside of Niamey, including attacks by armed bandits on foreign visitors. Thefts, robberies and residential break-ins are common; banditry, smuggling and other criminal activity in border areas.

Entry: Visa and yellow fever vaccination certificate needed.

Contact: No embassy in London, the nearest is Paris, www.nigeriafrance.com

Nigeria

Climate: Tropical; hot year-round. Rain falls mainly from April to July and September to October.

Safety: While the FCO doesn't advise against all travel, there are many areas of the country that shouldn't be entered, including the Niger Delta States, Akwa Ibon State and areas bordering Cameroon, where there's a high risk of kidnapping and armed robbery. Street crime like muggings and carjackings is common in Lagos. Localised outbreaks of civil unrest can occur at any time.

Entry: Visa needed.

Contact: www.nigeriahc.org.uk

Réunion

Climate: This Indian Ocean island has hot, wet summers from October to March and cooler, drier winters.

Safety: Low crime rate. The mosquito-borne Chikungunya virus continues to affect Réunion, increasing in summer and the rainy season.

Entry: An overseas department of France. No visa needed, but must have proof of onward journey.

Contact: http://france.embassy-uk.co.uk

Rwanda

Climate: Tropical and warm year-round. Highland regions are cooler. Rainy seasons run from March to May and October to December.

Safety: The FCO advises against all travel to the rural border areas with Democratic Republic of the Congo (DRC), except to the towns of Gisenyi, Kibuye and Cyangugu, because of the heavy military build-up on both sides of the border due to current fighting in North Kivu. Crime levels fairly low, though foreigners are targets for petty theft. Malaria and yellow fever common.

Entry: No visa needed.

Contact: www.ambarwanda.org.uk

Sao Tome & Principe

Climate: Hot and humid year-round; dry season July to August.

Safety: Crime rates low.

Entry: Visa needed before travel.

Contact: No embassy in the UK. Visa enquiries should be sent to Sao Tome Diplomatic Mission in Brussels: Square Montgomery, 175 Avenue de Tervuren, 1150 Brussels; Tel: 0032 2 734 89 66.

Senegal

Climate: Tropical; hot and humid. In the far south the rainy season runs from May to October, in the rest of the country it's from July to September.

Safety: The FCO advises against road travel in the Casamance region to the west of Kolda, other than on the main road from Ziguinchor to Cap Skiring, which is often used by groups of tourists. Petty theft common in Dakar.

Entry: No visa needed, proof of onward journey often required.

Contact: www.senegalembassy.co.uk

Seychelles

Climate: Tropical; hot, sunny and humid. Rains year-round but particularly November to April.
Safety: Low crime rate; some petty theft on beaches.
Entry: No visa needed.
Contact: http://ukinseychelles.fco.gov.uk/en

Sierra Leone

Climate: Hot and tropical year-round; rainy season from May to early November.
Safety: Fairly low crime rate; biggest risk to tourists is pick-pocketing and mugging in the capital Freetown. Rabies, lassa fever, waterborne diseases, malaria and other tropical diseases are common.
Entry: Visa needed before travel.
Contact: www.slhc-uk.org.uk

South Africa

Climate: South coast is hot and sunny and often windier in summer (October to March), and wet and cooler in winter. In the north, summers are hot and winters warm and sunny. The climate becomes more tropical the further east you go.
Safety: High crime levels, but these are mainly isolated to the townships away from tourist areas. Johannesburg is a crime hot spot, particularly carjacking, muggings and petty theft; be vigilant at airports, bus and railway stations. Avoid isolated beaches.
Entry: No visa needed.
Contact: http://southafrica.embassyhomepage.com

Sudan

Climate: Hot and arid, with much of the country desert. South is more humid and tropical, with some rain usual between April to November.

Safety: The FCO advises against all travel to these parts of Sudan: the Eritrean border, Abyei in South Kordofan, areas south of Juba in Central and East Equatoria and in West Equatoria within 40km (25 miles) of the border with the Democratic Republic of Congo (DRC). Volatile political situation. High threat of terrorism. Banditry in Darfur widespread.

Entry: Visa needed before travel. You have to register with the Aliens Department within three days of your arrival in the country regardless of whether you have a visa or not (two passport size photos are needed and the fee is the Dinar equivalent of around £15). Once registered, you don't have to buy an exit visa to leave the country. You have to get a permit before travelling outside of Khartoum and you must also register with the police at your new destination within 24 hours of arrival. If your passport has an Israeli visa or Israeli entry/exit stamps you will not be allowed to enter Sudan.

Contact: http://sudan.embassyhomepage.com

Swaziland

Climate: Hot and dry in the east, cooler and wetter on the high ground. Wet season runs from October to March.

Safety: High HIV/AIDS risk, with 43 per cent of the population infected. Avoid travelling in or out of Swaziland by road at night as there have been incidences of car hijacking. Low crime levels overall.

Entry: No visa needed for visits up to 30 days.

Contact: Swaziland Embassy, 020 7630 6611.

Tanzania

Climate: Tropical; very hot and humid in the lowlands, on the coast and in Zanzibar. Central plateau is semi-arid. Rainy season runs from March to May.

Safety: Underlying terrorism threat. Avoid travel to the area bordering Burundi and be wary in the Arusha region. Armed robberies aren't frequent, though on the increase in urban centres and remote tourist spots, such as Dar es Salaam and Zanzibar.

Entry: Visa needed; single-entry tourist visas can be obtained on arrival, but it's better to sort one out before you go. A yellow fever vaccination certificate is required from travellers coming from areas with a risk of yellow fever.

Contact: www.tanzania-online.gov.uk

Togo

Climate: Tropical; coastal regions hot and humid, interior drier. Rainy season runs from May to October.

Safety: The seafront area in capital Lomé is dangerous and should be avoided. Pickpocketing and theft are common, especially along the beach and in the market areas of the city. Rise in violent robberies and carjacking incidents targeting both foreigners and Togolese alike. Malaria and waterborne diseases are common.

Entry: Visa needed; available on arrival but FCO recommends getting one before you visit.

Contact: No embassy in the UK, contact Togolese Embassy to Paris at 8 Rue Alfred–Roll, 75017 Paris, 0033 1 43 80 12 13.

Tunisia

Climate: Mediterranean; hot, dry summers, mild, warm winters. Not much rain.

Safety: General terrorism threat. Avoid the border area with Algeria. Very little violent crime, but increase in petty theft like bag snatching in tourist areas.

Entry: No visa needed for stay of three months or less.

Contact: http://tunisia.embassyhomepage.com

Uganda

Climate: Mostly tropical, warm year-round. In the south, the rainy season runs from April to May, in the north it's from April to October. Cooler at altitude.

Safety: Underlying terrorism threat. The FCO advises against all travel to Karamoja region in northeastern Uganda (Kotido, Moroto, Nakapiripirit, Katakwi, Kaabong, Abim, Kapchorwa and Bukwa Districts) with the exception of trips to Kidepo Valley National Park, which should be made by air. Opportunist crime, like muggings and drive-by bag snatches, occur in the capital city Kampal.

Entry: Visa needed; avoid long queues at the airport and get one before you go.

Contact: www.ugandahighcommission.co.uk

Zambia

Climate: Tropical; wet season runs from November to May, hot and dry September to October.

Safety: Exercise caution when travelling in the rural parts of Northwestern, Copperbelt, Central and Luapula provinces close to the border with the Democratic Republic of Congo (DRC), particularly after dark. Risk of landmines on the Angola side of the Zambia/Angola border. Incidents of armed robberies and vehicle hijackings. In Lusaka, muggings, bag snatching and theft from parked cars are common in downtown areas, particularly near bus and railway stations and in some shopping areas. Avoid the Cairo Road area of the city, including Chachacha, Freedom Way and Lumumba Roads after dark. Malaria, rabies, TB, cholera and dysentery are common.

Entry: Visa needed; can be obtained on entry but it's best to get one prior to travel.

Contact: http://zambia.embassyhomepage.com

ASIA & MIDDLE EAST

Bahrain

Climate: Mild winters and very hot, humid summers. Ninety two per cent of the land is desert and dust storms are a common hazard.

Safety: Very low crime rate. Low terrorism threat.

Entry: No visa needed for British citizens.

Contact: www.bahrainembassy.london.co.uk

Bangladesh

Climate: Warm and tropical. Has yearly severe monsoons and cyclones, which last from March to June.

Safety: Flooding dangers, which also create health problems from contaminated water. Diseases such as malaria, dengue fever and leptospirosis are rife.

Entry: Visa required.

Contact: www.bangladeshhighcommission.org.uk

Bhutan

Climate: The southern plains are tropical, but the Himalayan region has severe winters and cool summers and is also an area of violent storms. Monsoon rains from June to August.

Safety: Low crime but watch out for signs of altitude sickness in the Himalayan areas.

Entry: Numbers of visitors is restricted. You must get a visa prior to visiting and all entry must be through a recognised travel agent. Certain areas also require an additional permit; prior authority is also needed to visit some religious buildings. There is also a fee of $200 per day for every day spent in Bhutan.

Contact: There is no British representation in Bhutan; the nearest consular office is the British Deputy High Commission in Kolkata (formerly Calcutta) in India. www.ukindia.fco.gov.uk

Brunei

Climate: Tropical and humid, with temperatures rarely dropping below 26°C all year. Monsoon from September to January.

Safety: Possession of drugs can result in the death penalty. Low terrorism threat; neighbouring Sabah has seen foreign nationals kidnapped with offshore islands and dive sites possible targets. Low crime rates. Dengue fever, but low malaria risk.

Entry: No visa needed for stays up to 30 days. Visas for longer stays can be obtained from the nearest Brunei diplomatic mission before you travel.

Contact: High Commission: 020 7581 0521

Burma

Climate: Very hot and humid with the risk of severe cyclones in the monsoon period, from April to October.

Safety: Repressive military regime frequently provokes violent demonstrations and riots. No accurate crime statistics, but muggings and petty thefts are a problem in Rangoon. Dengue fever, malaria and other waterborne disease are widespread.

Entry: Tourist visas are valid for four weeks and must be applied for before travel from the Burmese Embassy. You can only go to officially designated tourist areas and the Burmese government restricts much travel.

Contact: Embassy 020 7409 7043

Cambodia

Climate: Hot and tropical.

Safety: Street crime and muggings are a problem in Phnom Penh; beaches can be dangerous after dark. Malaria and dengue fever are widespread.

Entry: Visas needed, which can be obtained on arrival and at some border crossings. The 2009 price is $20 for a one-month stay.

Contact: www.cambodianembassy.org.uk

China

Climate: This vast country has climates which vary from sub-tropical to sub-arctic. The north has a continental climate, with winters from December to March. Typhoon season (May to August); storms can cause severe flooding.

Safety: Crimes against foreigners are rare. Earthquakes are a risk, with 70,000 people killed in the Sichuan Province in 2008 – the FCO still advises against travel in this region.

Entry: Visa required, although for mainland China not Hong Kong. Must be obtained prior to arrival. You also need to register your place of residence within 24 hours of arrival at the local Public Security Bureau, hotels will usually do this on your behalf. Visiting Hong Kong and returning to China requires a double visa to gain re-entry to the mainland.

Contact: www.chinese-embassy.org.uk

Georgia

Climate: Generally warm and pleasant, particularly along the Black Sea. Colder at altitude and sub-tropical on the coast.

Safety: Part of the old Soviet Union now in Southwest Asia. Has suffered from political tensions and the FCO advises not to travel to separatist regions like Ossetia. Crimes against foreigners low, no major health risks.

Entry: No visa required. UK passport permits up to 90-day stays, strongly recommended that British nationals register with the UK embassy.

Contact: www.geoemb.org.uk

Guam

Climate: Tropical, hot and humid year-round. Best time to visit is December to March which are the driest, coolest months.

Safety: Low terrorism threat, as Guam is an unincorporated USA territory with US Naval and Air Force bases. Low crime levels, although petty crime does occur.

Entry: No visa needed.

Contact: www.usembassy.org.uk

Hong Kong

Climate: Sub-tropical; hot, humid and wet summers, May to September, and cool but usually dry winters.

Safety: Violent crime levels very low, but petty theft and pick-pocketing occurs in urban areas. Isolated incidents of robberies in country parks. Dengue fever occurs.

Entry: Separate immigration controls from mainland China; you can stay for up to six months without a visa.

Contact: www.hketolondon.gov.hk

India

Climate: Varies according to which part of this vast country you're in. In general, most of the country has three seasons, hot, wet and cool. Monsoon season, May to July, brings rain to most of India. Pre-monsoon season is very hot in central India. Cooler in the north, with severe winters in mountain areas.

Safety: Terrorism threat throughout India; Mumbai was hit in 2008. The FCO advises against all travel to rural areas of Jammu and Kashmir, Manipur and Tripur and all travel to the border of Pakistan other than at the international border crossing of Wagah. Petty crime, such as handbag snatching, is on the rise in Delhi. Incidents of sexual assaults in Goa, Delhi and Rajasthan, so avoid walking alone in isolated places particularly after dark. Malaria and waterborne diseases common.

Entry: Visa needed before travel, if you arrive without one you'll be refused entry.

Contact: Indian High Commission, www.hcilondon.net/

Indonesia

Climate: Generally hot and humid across most of the islands, with tropical monsoons October to April.

Safety: High terrorism threat. The FCO advises against travel to Central Sulawesi Province and Maluku Province, where the political situation is unsettled, and advises caution about going to Aceh and Papua. Petty street crime and pickpocketings occur in urban areas. All airlines from Indonesia have been refused permission to enter the EU as they don't meet international safety standards. Risk of rabies in Bali, dengue and malaria throughout Indonesia.

Entry: Visa needed, though a tourist visa can be obtained on arrival for a short period.

Contact: www.indonesianembassy.org.uk

Israel

Climate: Warm, hot summers, particularly July and August; mild winters with rainfall mainly occurring in December and February.

Safety: High risk of terrorism. Conflict and violence occur rapidly and unpredictably around the Gaza strip and security in the West Bank remains volatile; do not travel to either region (apart from Bethlehem, Jericho and the Jordan Valley). Theft of passports and valuables from public beaches is common.

Entry: No visa needed.

Contact: www.israel.embassyhomepage.com

Japan

Climate: Temperate; warm spring, hot, humid summers with rain and cold winters, though in the north it can get very cold with plenty of snow.

Safety: Low rates of common crime, such as mugging. The country has a very severe zero tolerance for drugs, and possession of even small amounts can result in prison. Japan is vulnerable to natural disasters, including earthquakes, typhoons and tidal waves.

Entry: No visa needed. Since November 2007, all foreign visitors entering Japan must be fingerprinted and digitally photographed during entry procedures. Those refusing to be fingerprinted or photographed will be denied entry.

Contact: www.japan.embassyhomepage.com

Jordan

Climate: Eastern valleys are hot and dry with little rain. West is milder and wetter, though still warm. Desert areas have very hot summers, cold winters and little rain.

Safety: General terrorism threat. Crime levels low, although solo women travellers should cover up and avoid situations where they might be a victim of sexual assault as incidents have occurred involving tourists in the past.

Entry: Visa needed. You can get a single entry visa, valid for one month on arrival. You can extend your visa for up to three months at a police station.

Contact: www.jordan.embassyhomepage.com

Kazakhstan

Climate: Dry, with very hot summer and cold winters. Arid desert in the south and very low temperatures in the northern steppes.

Safety: Underlying terrorism threat. Some parts of the country are closed territories and require advance permission to enter. Muggings and theft occur in cities and rural areas, and tourists are targeted. Robberies reported on trains, so lock railway compartments.

Entry: Visa needed prior to travel, usually valid for 30 days from date of issue.

Contact: www.kazembassy.org.uk

Kuwait

Climate: Very hot, dry summers (April to September); cooler in winter. A desert climate with little rainfall.

Safety: General terrorism threat and the FCO advises to keep a high level of security awareness at all times. Zero tolerance for drug possession and trafficking and penalty can include the death sentence. Violent crime against foreigners is rare.

Entry: Visa needed, which can be obtained on arrival and lasts up to 90 days. You need a return air ticket.

Contact: www.britishembassy-kuwait.org/

Kyrgyzstan

Climate: Harsh, with very hot dry summers and very cold winters. Rainfall is low. Mountains have year-round snow.

Safety: Terrorism threat. Border tensions mean you should only use officially recognized crossings as there's a risk of landmines. Mugging and sometimes violent theft regularly occur in cities and rural areas.

Entry: Visa needed; you can obtain one-month visas on arrival or in advance.

Contact: www.kyrgyz-embassy.org.uk

Laos

Climate: Hot year-round in most of the country. Monsoon rains from May to October. Temperatures in the highland areas are lower and can drop to freezing in December and January.

Safety: Violent crime is on the increase and passport theft is a particular problem. There have been reports of drug-laced food and drink, so be wary of accepting drinks from strangers. Drug possession or trafficking can result in the death sentence.

Entry: Visa needed and the regulations change constantly, so contact the nearest embassy (Paris) before travel.

Contact: www.laoparis.com

Lebanon

Climate: Hot, dry summers, mild winters (November to February); humid on the coast.

Safety: Until recently, it was recommended that no Brits travel to Lebanon unless essential due to the high threat of terrorism. That advice has now changed as the situation is now calm, but it's still advisable not to travel to Palestinian camps, Tripoli and south of Litani. Very low crime rate against tourists, although bag snatching is on the increase.

Entry: Visa needed; tourist visit visa can be obtained on arrival.

Contact: www.lebanon.embassyhomepage.com

Macao

Climate: Sub-tropical; hot, humid and wet summers, cool, drier winters. Typhoon season: July to August.

Safety: Low crime rate against tourists, but watch out for pick-pocketing in crowded areas. Dengue fever common.

Entry: Part of the People's Republic of China, but has retained its own immigration controls and at present no visa is needed.

Contact: www.chinese-embassy.org.uk

Malaysia

Climate: Tropical; hot, sunny and very humid year-round.

Safety: Foreigners have been kidnapped in the past in East

Malaysia; boats travelling to offshore islands and dive sites are possible targets so exercise caution, particularly around Eastern Sabah. Zero tolerance on drugs; possession of tiny quantities can lead to prison and the death penalty. Bag snatching common, particularly by thieves on motorbikes. Be wary of gambling scams and spiked drinks in bars. Credit card and ATM fraud is widespread.

Entry: No visa needed. UK citizens travelling from Peninsular Malaysia to East Malaysia (Sabah and Sarawak) need to carry their passports to enter East Malaysia.

Contact: www.malaysia.embassyhomepage.com

Maldives

Climate: Hot and humid year-round, but sea breezes moderate the temperature which rarely dips below 24–33°C. Monsoon season April to November, sunniest months October to May.

Safety: Underlying terrorism threat. Crime levels low; petty theft on beaches and hotel rooms does occur though, so take care of valuables.

Entry: Visa needed; can be obtained on arrival and valid for 30 days provided you have a ticket to continue your journey after the Maldives.

Contact: www.maldiveshighcommission.org

Marshall Islands

Climate: Warm and humid year-round, cooled by trade winds. Driest, coolest months are January to March. Southern islands get more rain.

Safety: Very low crime, only a handful of British tourists visit each year and it's usually trouble-free.

Entry: No visa needed for visits up to 30 days.

Contact: No MI embassy in UK and vice versa. For advice, go to http://ukinthephilippines.fco.gov.uk

Mongolia

Climate: ontinental; mild summers (June to August), long, very cold winters with plenty of snow.

Safety: Relatively safe; violent muggings and petty crime does occur in Ulaanbaatar. Avoid going out alone here on foot at night; use clearly identifiable and inexpensive taxis. Travelling by road can be difficult as there's little infrastructure; take a satellite phone and GPS in case of emergencies.

Entry: Visa needed before travel.

Contact: www.embassyofmongolia.co.uk

Nepal

Climate: Dry and sunny for most of the year, apart from the monsoon season from July to October. Arctic conditions on the mountain peaks; best time for trekking is October to November and February to April.

Safety: Terrorism threat, including bombings and shootings. Volatile political situation; avoid demonstrations. Trekking problems include extortion money, where tourists are forced to pay 'taxes' along the route, and disreputable companies and guide. Altitude sickness can be a problem, acclimatise slowly. Monsoon rains can cause flooding and landslides.

Entry: Visa needed.

Contact: www.npembassy.org.uk

North Korea

Climate: Continental; warm summers, cold winters with snow in the north. Most rain falls during the summer months.

Safety: Crime against foreigners is very unusual.

Entry: Visa needed. You must register with the Ministry of Foreign Affairs if your visit is for more than 24 hours. It's not possible to enter the Democratic People's Republic of Korea (DPRK) (North Korea) from the Republic of Korea (ROK) (South Korea).

Contact: Embassy of the DPRK, 020 8992 4965

Oman

Climate: Very hot, particularly in the north. Monsoon rains fall in the southern uplands from June to September. Coast is more humid than the interior.

Safety: Very little crime against foreigners. Underlying terrorism threat. Reports of sexual harassment; it's a Muslim country so cover up in public areas.

Entry: Visa needed; can obtain on entry.

Contact: www.omanembassy.org.uk

Pakistan

Climate: Warm year-round in most areas; can be cooler in the Hindu Kush. Wettest months are June to August. December to February is warm and sunny, with cooler nights.

Safety: High terrorism risk and the FCO advises against all travel to the Federally Administered Tribal Areas, Northern and Western Balochistan and much of North West Frontier Province (NWFP) including the Frontier Regions of Peshawar, Kobat, Tank, Banu, Lakki and Dera Ismail Khan. Criminal violence, including armed carjacking, robbery, kidnap and murder, is common, especially in Karachi. If you want to travel here, you're strongly recommended to register with the British High Commission.

Entry: Visa needed.

Contact: www.phclondon.org

Palau

Climate: Tropical oceanic climate; warm and humid year-round. Dry season is February to April.

Safety: Very few British tourists visit; virtually no crime. Dengue
             fever occurs here.

Entry: No visa needed.

Contact: No embassy in the UK; consular contact
             http://ukinthephilippines.fco.gov.uk

Papua New Guinea

Climate: Tropical; hot and humid year-round. Cooler in the
             highlands, which can have snow. Lots of rain, partic-
             ularly December to March.

Safety: Serious crime is particularly high in the capital, Port
             Moresby, and in the cities of Lae and Mt Hagen. Armed
             carjackings and robberies are common in all three
             cities. Sporadic outbreaks of tribal fighting are a normal
             occurrence, especially in the Highlands Provinces,
             particularly the Southern and Western Highlands and
             Enga Provinces. Threat from natural disasters including
             volcanic eruptions, earthquakes and tsunamis.

Entry: Visa needed; can obtain on arrival.

Contact: www.pnghighcomm.org.uk

Philippines

Climate: Mostly warm and humid. Hot and sunny in the wet
             season, May to October, when the islands can get
             torrential rain.

Safety: High terrorism threat throughout the country. The FCO
             advises against travel to mainland Mindanao and
             the Sulu archipelago because of ongoing terrorist
             and insurgent activity. High incidence of street crime
             and robberies.

Entry: No visa needed for stays up to 21 days; for longer
             periods you can apply for a tourist visa.

Contact: Philippines Embassy in London, 020 7451 1800.

Qatar

Climate: Very hot, temperatures can hit 50 degrees. Desert climate with little rainfall. Best time to visit is November or February to early March when it's cooler.

Safety: General terrorism threat. Low crime rate; women should take care travelling alone at night.

Entry: Visa needed; single entry short stay visa can be purchased at the airport on arrival. Once in Qatar you can extend your stay through the Immigration Authorities for a further 14 days.

Contact: www.qatar.embassyhomepage.com

Saudi Arabia

Climate: Very hot, particularly in the summer months from April to October. Humidity low. The coast gets some rain, but overall very dry.

Safety: High threat of terrorism. Crime rate is very low and not usually a problem for travellers. Women must cover up and it is illegal for them to drive; possession of alcohol can result in prison sentences and possession of drugs the death penalty.

Entry: Visa needed.

Contact: www.saudiarabia.embassyhomepage.com

Singapore

Climate: Hot, sunny and humid year-round. Rain falls year-round, wettest months October and November to January.

Safety: Violent crime is rare, petty theft more common. Dengue fever risk. Drug possession of any kind can result in the death penalty.

Entry: No visa needed for stays up to 30 days.

Contact: www.mfa.gov.sg/london/

South Korea

Climate: Winters are dry, sunny and very cold; summers are hot, wet and humid; typhoon season can run from June to November.

Safety: Crime rate low; higher rate of petty theft like pick-pocketing and assault in cities like Seoul and Busan. Zero tolerance on drugs, you can be detained on the basis of a drugs test even if you don't possess any.

Entry: No visa required for visits of up to 90 days with a valid UK passport.

Contact: www.korean.embassyhomepage.com

Sri Lanka

Climate: Tropical; hot summers, warm winters and rain year-round. High humidity. The southwest monsoon brings rain from May to August in Colombo. Northeast monsoon from November to February.

Safety: High terrorism threat. The FCO advises against all travel to the north and eastern areas of the island. Violent crime against foreigners is rare; petty theft occurs particularly in cities.

Entry: Visa needed; 30-day visa available on arrival.

Contact: www.slhclondon.org

Syria

Climate: Varied. Mediterranean on the coast. The steppe regions are warmer with less rain. Snow in the mountains in the winter. Southeast is arid desert.

Safety: Terrorism threat. Crime levels are low, passport theft is on the increase. Drug possession of any kind is life imprisonment, trafficking is the death penalty. Cover up; Syria is a Muslim country and women have been attacked for not wearing Islamic dress.

Entry: Visa needed. If your passport contains an Israeli stamp or stamps from other countries' border crossing points with Israel, you will be refused entry.

Contact: www.syria.embassyhomepage.com

Taiwan

Climate: Tropical monsoon; hot and humid in summer, typhoons likely from July to September. Monsoon rains fall between June to August, particularly in mountain regions.

Safety: Very low crime rate, with only small-scale petty crime very occasionally affecting tourists. Dengue fever common in southern Taiwan.

Entry: No visa needed for visits of up to 30 days.

Contact: www.taiwanembassy.org.uk/

Tajikistan

Climate: Continental to sub-tropical. Warm summers and cold winters in lower western areas. Cold winters in the mountains.

Safety: Tourism, health and transport infrastructure very poor. Avoid off-road areas immediately adjoining the Afghan, Uzbek and Kyrgyz borders, which may be mined. General terrorism threat. Armed incidents occur between border forces and drug traffickers along the Afghan border. There have been occasional muggings and petty crime against foreigners, but Dushanbe is a relatively safe city.

Entry: Visa needed prior to entry.

Contact: www.tajembassy.org.uk

Thailand

Climate: Hot and humid year-round, particularly during the monsoon season, which runs from May to October in most of the country. The further south you go, the wetter it is.

Safety: Volatile political situation and high terrorism threat. The FCO advises against all but essential travel to, or through, the far southern provinces of Pattani, Yala, Narathiwat and Songkhla. There continue to be frequent attacks, including bombing and shooting, due to insurgency and civil unrest in these areas. Penalties for drug possession include the death penalty. Most crime is opportunist. There have been incidents of tourists having their drinks spiked in bars, and credit card fraud is common. Sexual assaults have become prevalent in the Koh Samui archipelago. All travel to the Thailand/Cambodia border region is discouraged due to sporadic fighting.

Entry: No visa required for visits of up to 30 days.

Contact: www.thaiembassyuk.org.uk

Turkmenistan

Climate: Arid desert, very hot in summer but below freezing in winter.

Safety: Low crime rate, occasional mugging or theft.

Entry: British nationals require a visa to enter Turkmenistan. A Letter of Invitation, certified by the State Migration Service of Turkmenistan is needed from a private individual or company to support the visa application. For tourists, these can be obtained from authorised travel agents.

Contact: http://ukinturkmenistan.fco.gov.uk/en

United Arab Emirates

Climate: Hot year-round. Wet season from November to February. Cooler in May to October.

Safety: Terrorism threat. Low crime rate, street crime very rare. It's a punishable offence to drink alcohol or be drunk in public, but you can get alcohol in hotel bars.

Entry: No visa needed.

Contact: www.uaeembassyuk.net

Uzbekistan

Climate: Very hot summers, cold winters; dry and arid.

Safety: The FCO advises against all but essential travel to areas bordering Afghanistan, Tajikistan and Kyrgyzstan other than via authorised crossing points. General terrorism threat. Occasional muggings and petty crimes against foreigners.

Entry: Visa needed prior to travel.

Contact: www.uzbekembassy.org/

Vietnam

Climate: In the north summers, between May and September are very hot, with plenty of rain while winters from November to March are cooler (around 25°C) and drier. In the south it's also tropical, but warm near constant temperature year-round (25°C).

Safety: Crime levels low, although petty crime increasing in larger cities. Dengue fever and malaria risk. Drug trafficking and possession carries heavy penalties, including the death penalty.

Entry: Visa needed prior to entry; usually valid for one month. Do not overstay as this can result in a fine or imprisonment.

Contact: www.vietnamembassy.org.uk/

AUSTRALIA & OCEANIA

Australia

Climate: Huge climate range from tropical Queensland rain-forests, to the vast inner desert areas and temperate Tasmania. Beware of tropical cyclones in the Queensland and Northern Territory areas between November and April. Bush fires are also a risk in high summer (November to February).

Safety: Generally good. Crime levels are fairly low and mainly in the major cities. Your biggest risk is the great outdoors – there were 100 drownings and 10,000 beach rescues recorded in 2007!

Entry: A visa is required before arrival.

Contact: The Australian High Commission, www.ukembassy.gov.au

Fiji

Climate: Tropical, with high temperatures all year. Wettest months are November to December and March to April. Cyclone risk from November to April.

Safety: Low crime levels. Occasional outbreaks of dengue fever and typhoid. Zero drugs tolerance; mandatory prison sentence for possession.

Entry: No visa needed and UK passport allows you to stay for up to four months.

Contact: www.fijihighcommission.org.uk

French Polynesia

Climate: Hot and humid, sunny year-round. Drier and cooler months from May to October.

Safety: Low crime rate. Low rate of typhoid. Your biggest risk is sunburn!

Entry: No visa needed but you must have a return air ticket.

Contact: www.amafrance-uk.org

Kiribati

Climate: Central islands have a maritime equatorial climate. Northern and southern islands are tropical, with warm temperatures year-round and low rainfall.

Safety: Very low crime rate.

Entry: No visa needed.

Contact: N/A

Nauru

Climate: Tropical; hot year-round. Best time to visit, November to March.

Safety: Crime rate very low; no history of serious civil unrest. Make sure you have comprehensive healthcare as serious injury or illness require air evacuation to Guam or Australia which is very expensive.

Entry: Visa needed, plus proof of onward journey; can obtain visa on arrival, valid for 30 days.

Contact: No UK embassy. South Pacific Tourism Organisation, www.south-pacific.travel

New Caledonia

Climate: Temperate year-round; warm and humid November to February, cooler July and August.

Safety: Very low crime; be wary of tropical cyclones mid-December to mid-March.

Entry: A dependent territory of France; no visa required.

Contact: www.france.embassy-uk.co.uk

New Zealand

Climate: Temperate. Far north is sub-tropical, with mild winters and warm summers. Wettest months are May to August, best time to visit spring/summer months, November to March.

Safety: Low crime levels, however there is pickpocketing and other street crime in towns and cities, and a rise in thefts from hire cars/camper vans in major tourist areas.

Entry: No visa required, can visit for up to six months on a UK passport.

Contact: www.nzembassy.com

Samoa

Climate: Hot and humid year-round. Cyclone season December to April, which are also the hottest months.

Safety: Serious crime rates are very low; occasional petty theft.
Entry: No visa needed.
Contact: No UK embassy, visit www.samoa.co.uk

Solomon Islands

Climate: Tropical; summer, November to April, is wet, hot and humid, and is also the cyclone season. Best time to go are winter months, May to December.
Safety: Civil unrest, and foreigners have been a target for violence. Pickpocketing and harassment occur around ATMs. Don't wander around Honiara alone at night. Dengue fever and malaria risk.
Entry: No visa needed.
Contact: www.solomonislands.embassy.gov.au

Tonga

Climate: Tropical oceanic; warm and hot year-round. Heavy rains from February to March.
Safety: Petty crime on the increase; occasional incidences of violent assault. Dengue fever risk.
Entry: No visa needed for visits up to 30 days. Yellow fever certificate is required by all travellers over one year old who have been in an infected area prior to arrival in Tonga.
Contact: Tonga High Commission, 020 7724 5828.

Tuvalu

Climate: Hot and humid year-round, lots of rain, particularly November to February.
Safety: Only a handful of tourists visit this tiny Polynesian island nation each year and it's virtually trouble-free.
Entry: No visa needed.
Contact: Consulate of Tuvalu, 020 8879 0985.

Vanuatu

Climate: Tropical; north hotter and rainier than the south. Dry season runs from May to October.

Safety: The biggest risk here is volcanic activity, plus earthquakes; check with the tourist office for latest reports before visiting any of the islands. Fairly low crime rates, although street crime is on the increase.

Entry: No visa needed; proof of onward journey required.

Contact: No Vanuatu embassy in UK, contact Vanuatu Consulate in Paris: 9, rue Daru, 75008 Paris, +33 1 40 53 82 25.

EUROPE

Albania

Climate: The coast and plains enjoy a Mediterranean climate in contrast to the mountainous interior, which has hot summers and long snowy winters.

Safety: This is one of Europe's poorest countries and law and order remains a problem; high levels of organised crime and corruption. The FCO advises against all travel to the north-eastern border areas.

Entry: British citizens can go for 30 days without a visa, after this period you'll need to apply for an extension for up to 60 days.

Contact: www.albanianembassy.co.uk

Andorra

Climate: Warm in summer months; great for snow sports in winter.

Safety: One of the smallest and most beautiful countries in Europe, there's very little crime. Strict zero tolerance on drugs.

Entry: No visa needed.

Contact: Andorra Embassy, 020 8874 4806.

Austria

Climate: Can be very hot in summer and very cold and snowy in winter.

Safety: Low crime rate and low terrorism risk. There are avalanche dangers in the mountains in winter months; risk of pickpocketing and muggings in Vienna. Heavy penalties for drug possession and trafficking.

Entry: No visa required.

Contact: www.austria.embassyhomepage.com

Belarus

Climate: Continental with warm summers and cold winters with lots of snow.

Safety: Formally part of the old Soviet Union; threat of terrorism and crime is fairly low. Things to be aware of include severe penalties for the possession and use of drugs and a threat of theft on sleeper trains from Warsaw to Moscow. There's also a risk of contaminated foodstuffs, such as local dairy produce, and water from wells, as a result of contamination from the Chernobyl disaster.

Entry: Complicated. Visas are needed, including travel by train from Warsaw, Moscow, Kiev and St Petersburg. There is a $300 fine for travelling without a visa. Anyone staying more than three days must register with the local police station (OUIR), plus you need to complete a migration card to enter and leave the country, which must be stamped at the local OUIR office.

Contact: Embassy of the Republic of Belarus, 020 7937 3288, www.uk.belembassy.org

Belgium

Climate: Similar to the UK, warm summers, cold winters with rain throughout the year.

Safety: Low crime rate.

Entry: No visa needed.

Contact: www.diplomatie.be/london

Bosnia and Herzegovina

Climate: Pleasantly warm in summer, winters can be harsh with lots of snow at altitude.

Safety: Part of the old Yugoslavia and still recovering from the Balkan wars of the 90s. Ethnic tension remains, as do some unexploded landmines in the more remote rural mountain areas so seek local advice. Crime levels low against foreigners, but be vigilant against pickpockets in Sarajevo. Rare cases of rabies in wild animals or stray dogs. UK has reciprocal healthcare agreements, but this doesn't cover extreme sports so check your health insurance.

Entry: No visa needed. Stays limited to 90 days with a six-month period. All foreign nationals must register with the police within 48 hours of arrival in the country – hotels will usually arrange this.

Contact: www.bhembassy.co.uk

Bulgaria

Climate: Very hot in the summer and cold and snowy in the winter, particularly in the mountains.

Safety: There is a lot of organised crime and gangs, but this rarely impacts on tourists.

Entry: No visa required. Note, Bulgaria is still emerging from the communist era and is still largely a cash economy with credit cards not yet widely accepted.

Contact: www.bulgarianembassy.org.uk

Croatia

Climate: Warm Mediterranean climate along the coast for much of the year; inland in the winter it can get very cold with lots of snow.

Safety: Following the turbulent break up of Yugoslavia and ethnic fighting, it's now politically stable and is a prosperous country with low crime levels and no major health threats. Unexploded mines from the war years are still a danger, particularly in isolated mountains areas, so trekkers should always go with a guide.

Entry: No visa needed.
Contact: http://uk.mfa.hr/

Cyprus

Climate: Summers are hot and dry. Winters are mild, though snow on mountains.

Safety: The island remains divided between Greece and Turkey and UN forces still patrol the buffer zone. However, the political situation is calm and more than a million Brits visit each year without incident. Crime is very low and there are no real health concerns. The biggest problem on the island at the moment is water shortages in the summer months, which has led to restrictions in hotels.

Entry: No visa needed. However, as a British national, you can't fly directly from the UK to the Turkish Cypriot northern area; you can cross the green line into either section but only at official checkpoints and you will need to show your passport.

Contact: www.mfa.gov.cy/

Czech Republic

Climate: A continental climate with warm summers and cold winters, with temperatures below freezing and thick fogs likely.

Safety: Petty theft and pickpocketing occurs at major tourist sites, particularly in Prague; no major health risks.

Entry: No visa needed.
Contact: www.czechembassy.org.uk

Denmark

Climate: Temperate climate, much like the UK; can get quite cold in January/February.

Safety: Crime rates are very low; no health problems and reciprocal healthcare agreements exist between Denmark and the UK.

Entry: UK passport means you can stay for up to three months.

Contact: www.amblondon.um.dk/en

Estonia

Climate: Warm, temperate summers; winters can be very cold with snow likely December to March.

Safety: Low crime rates, although petty theft has increased in tourist hot spots like Tallinn.

Entry: No visa needed; UK passport allows you to stay for up to 90 days.

Contact: www.estonia.gov.uk

Finland

Climate: A quarter of the country lies north of the Arctic circle, so expect very cold temperatures sometimes are low as – 30 degrees, lots of snow and little daylight in the winter. Short, warm summers.

Safety: Very low crime levels and no health risks apart from the severe cold in winter.

Entry: No visa needed.

Contact: www.finemb.org.uk

France

Climate: Temperate in the north; warm summers, cold and frosty winters. The south has a Mediterranean climate, with hot summers and mild winters with little rain.

Safety: Crime levels and types of crimes are similar to the UK. No real health risks.

Entry: No visa needed.

Contact: www.ambafrance-uk.org

Germany

Climate: Temperate in the north and central regions, with mild summers and cold winters. East is colder. Rains year-round.

Safety: Crime levels generally low and no major health risks.

Entry: No visa needed.

Contact: www.germanembassy.co.uk

Greece

Climate: Mediterranean, with hot, dry summers and mild, wet winters.

Safety: Low threat of domestic terrorism. Around three million Brits visit Greece each year largely without incident, however there have been riots and violence in Athens recently and so visitors should avoid areas where demonstrations are taking place. Petty theft is common in tourist hot spots.

Entry: No visa needed. UK passport allows visits for up to three months.

Contact: www.greekembassy.org.uk

Greenland

Climate: Arctic climate. Often windy and in summer temperatures are around 1-20°C. In the winter they go as low as –50°C in the north.

Safety: Very low crime rate and no major health risks, apart from the cold.

Entry: No visa needed. A self-governing island region of Denmark, so information can be found at the Danish embassy.

Contact: www.amblondon.um.dk/en

Hungary

Climate: Temperate; warm summers from June to August and very cold winters.

Safety: Fairly low crime rates. Pickpocketing is common in Budapest, particularly at tourist hot spots. No major health risks.

Entry: No visa needed.

Contact: www.mfa.gov.hu/emb/london

Iceland

Climate: Very cold winters; short, cool summers.

Safety: Low crime, although petty theft and alcohol-related incidents do occur in Reykjavik.

Entry: No visa needed; you can stay up to three months with a valid British passport.

Contact: www.iceland.org/uk

Italy

Climate: Mostly Mediterranean; warm summers and mild winters. The northern Alpine region gets very cold winters with plenty of snow. In the south there's little rain.

Safety: Low levels of crime in rural areas, higher in cities. Petty crime, such as pickpockets and bag snatching common in major cities, particularly Rome.

Entry: No visa needed.

Contact: Italian embassy, 020 7312 2200.

Latvia

Climate: Very cold winters (November to February) with snow likely December to March; warm summers.

Safety: Low crime levels, but has been an increase in tourist muggings and credit card fraud. Recent increase in hepatitis A cases, so get vaccinated before arrival.

Entry: No visa needed.

Contact: www.ukinlatvia.fco.gov.uk

Liechtenstein

Climate: Temperate; warm, dry summers and cold winters.

Safety: Very low crime rate, but still be vigilant against pickpockets in city centres and other public places like rail stations. If you're in the Alps in winter, there's a moderate danger of avalanches.

Entry: No visa needed.

Contact: The Swiss embassy represents Liechtenstein in the UK; www.switzerland.embassyhomepage.com

Lithuania

Climate: Temperate; warm summers and cold winters. Rain year-round.

Safety: Low crime rate but risk of petty theft in cities and on public transport. Risk of rabies and tick-borne encephalitis in forested areas.

Entry: No visa needed.

Contact: www.lithuania.embassyhomepage.com

Luxembourg

Climate: Temperate; warm summers and cold winters with heavy snow in highland areas.

Safety: Low crime rate, no major health risks.

Entry: No visa needed.

Contact: http://ukinluxembourg.fco.gov.uk/en/

Macedonia

Climate: Hot summers, cold winters, wet springs and dry autumns.

Safety: Most areas are trouble-free, but there is sporadic violence in the northwest and Skopje as armed gangs operate here, so avoid these areas. You have to get permission from a local police station to access the areas bordering Serbia. Credit card fraud is widespread.

Entry: No visa needed.

Contact: www.macedonia.embassyhomepage.com

Malta

Climate: Mediterranean; hot, dry summers, mild winters.
Safety: Crime against tourists is rare, although handbag snatching and theft from parked cars does occasionally occur.
Entry: No visa needed.
Contact: www.malta.embassyhomepage.com

Moldova

Climate: Warm summers, mild winters; moderate rainfall year-round.
Safety: You should be alert to the risk of street crime and petty theft, particularly in Chisinau, and for pickpockets and bag snatchers in crowded areas. Credit card and ATM fraud is on the increase and you should avoid using credit/debit cards whenever possible.
Entry: No visa needed.
Contact: www.moldovanembassy.org.uk

Monaco

Climate: Mediterranean; hot, dry summers and mild winters. Little rain.
Safety: Street crime is rare, no major health risks.
Entry: No visa needed.
Contact: france.embassy-uk.co.uk

Netherlands

Climate: Similar to the UK.
Safety: Pickpocketing and bag snatching are common in Amsterdam. Don't carry or use drugs. The Netherlands has a reputation for being tolerant on the use of soft drugs, but in reality it's only allowed in certain areas of major cities; elsewhere possession can lead to a prison sentence.
Entry: No visa needed.
Contact: www.netherlands-embassy.org.uk

Norway

Climate: Warm summers, cold, snowy winters. Milder on the coast, rain throughout the year, heaviest from June to October.

Safety: Low crime rates, although petty theft does occur, particularly at airports and railway stations around Oslo.

Entry: No visa needed.

Contact: www.norway.org.uk

Poland

Climate: Continental; very cold winters from December to March; hot summers, particularly on the coast.

Safety: Violent crime is rare, but there is a risk of robbery on rail and bus journeys. Pickpocketing occurs in cities.

Entry: No visa needed.

Contact: www.poland.embassyhomepage.com

Portugal

Climate: Warm summers, mild winters. Cooler in the north. Not much rain, mainly falls December to March.

Safety: Low levels of crime, but pickpocketing, bag snatching and theft from cars is on the increase in cities. Take care of valuables on the beach.

Entry: No visa needed.

Contact: www.portugal.embassyhomepage.com

Romania

Climate: Continental; hot summers, particularly the Black Sea coast. Winters, December to March, are very cold and snowy.

Safety: Most tourist visits are trouble-free. Petty theft, particularly in Bucharest, is fairly common. Rabies occurs mainly in rural areas.

Entry: No visa needed.

Contact: www.romania.embassyhomepage.com

Russian Federation

Climate: Such a vast country has a very varied climate. Northern and Central European Russia: mildest areas are along the Baltic coast. Summer sunshine may be nine hours a day, but winters can be very cold. Siberia: Very cold winters, but summers can be pleasant, although they tend to be short and wet. Southern European Russia: Winter is shorter than in the north. Steppes (in the southeast) have hot, dry summers and very cold winters. The north and northeastern Black Sea has mild winters, but heavy rainfall year-round.

Safety: General terrorism threat and the FCO advises against all travel to Chechnya, Ingushetia and Dagestan. Petty crime occurs in most Russian cities, with St Petersburg seeing a sharp increase in street crime.

Entry: Visa needed. During periods of high demand, like summer holidays, you should apply for your visa well in advance (they can normally be processed in 15 days).

Contact: www.rusemblon.org

Serbia

Climate: Continental; warm summers and cold winters with snow. Steady rain.

Safety: Serbia rejects Kosovo's declaration of independence, but the UK along with other EU member states recognises it. There are still landmines around the Presevo and Bujanovac districts in south Serbia. Street crime in cities occurs.

Entry: No visa needed for stays up to 90 days. The Serbian government doesn't recognise entry points from Kosovo or those on Kosovo's external borders with Albania, Macedonia or Montenegro.

Contact: www.serbianembassy.org.uk

Slovakia

Climate: Continental; warm summers and cold winters with snow. Steady rain.

Safety: Risk of petty theft in Bratislava, particularly pickpocketing in tourist hot spots. You must carry your passport with you at all times as identification, so keep it safe.

Entry: No visa required.

Contact: www.slovakembassy.co.uk

Slovenia

Climate: Continental; warm summers and cold winters with snow in the mountains. Mediterranean on the coast.

Safety: Low crime, mainly petty theft from tourists.

Entry: No visa needed.

Contact: www.slovenia.embassyhomepage.com

Spain

Climate: Hotter and drier in the south. Temperate in the north. Little rain, mild winters.

Safety: Terrorism threat from Basque terrorist organisation. Street crime in main tourist areas, particularly muggings and pickpocketing.

Entry: No visa needed.

Contact: www.spain.embassyhomepage.com

Sweden

Climate: Mild in the south. Plenty of rainfall year-round. Stockholm has cold winters and warm summers. Long winters in the north and lots of snow.

Safety: Very low crime. Pickpocketing in major cities, with tourists targeted. Very severe winters, so you need to be prepared for harsh conditions.

Entry: No visa needed.

Contact: www.sweden.embassyhomepage.com

Switzerland

Climate: Seasons similar to the UK, although summers tend to be warmer and winters colder. Very cold with plenty of snow in the mountains in winter.

Safety: Very low crime rate, pickpockets operate in city centres and on public transport. Moderate danger of avalanches throughout the year in the Alpine regions.

Entry: No visa needed.

Contact: www.switzerland.embassyhomepage.com

Turkey

Climate: Mediterranean on the coast, more extreme inland, with hot dry summers and very cold, snowy winters. Wettest months are December to February.

Safety: Terrorism threat; attacks usually carried out in the southeast by separatist Kurdistan Workers Party (PKK). FCO advises against all but essential travel to the provinces of Hakkari, Sirnak, Siirt and Tunceli. Low crime rate, but street robbery and pickpocketing do occur in major tourist areas of Istanbul. Occasional incidences of rape of foreigners, the majority of which happen in the coastal tourist areas in the southwest; don't walk around alone on beaches at night.

Entry: Visa needed; can be obtained on arrival and is valid for 90 days.

Contact: turkishembassylondon.org

Ukraine

Climate: Continental; warm summers, cool winters with regular snow fall. The coast has a more Mediterranean climate, with milder winters.

Safety: Petty crime common in tourist hot spots. Higher levels of crime in Kiev, including muggings and violent attacks on foreigners.

Entry: No visa needed.

Contact: www.ukraine.embassyhomepage.com

NORTH & CENTRAL AMERICA

Antigua & Barbuda

Climate: Fabulous year-round and the sunniest island in the archipelagos boasting eight-and-a-half hours of sunlight every day. Temperatures rarely drop below mid-70s. There is a hurricane season from June to November.

Safety: Very low crime rates.

Entry: No visa needed.

Contact: www.antigua-barbuda.com

Bahamas

Climate: Enjoys a sunny, sub-tropical climate year-round.

Safety: Low crime.

Entry: No visa required.

Contact: www.bahamas.co.uk

Barbados

Climate: Delightful warm, sub-tropical climate year-round.

Safety: Relatively safe, with fairly low crime. Make sure you have health insurance before you travel as medical treatment can be very expensive.

Entry: No visa required.

Contact: Barbados High Commission, 020 7323 6872.

Belize

Climate: Hot, humid and tropical. Rainforests in the south are very wet; can get cool at night in the mountains. Rainy season runs May to October and hurricane season June to November.

Safety: Mugging is a risk for foreigners, particularly in Belize city. Dengue fever is prevalent, so take precautions.

Entry: British nationals can visit for up to 30 days without a visa.

Contact: www.tralbelize.org

Bermuda

Climate: Beautiful warm climate year-round; hurricane season from June to November.

Safety: Moderate crime rate, most visits to the island are trouble-free.

Entry: No visa needed, but accommodation must be booked before arrival. Note, there's no British embassy or consular representation on the island.

Contact: www.gov.bm

British Virgin Islands

Climate: Warm year-round, hurricane season from June to November.

Safety: Very low crime rate. Make sure you have full medical insurance as facilities are limited and serious problems require air evacuation to the mainland USA which costs a fortune. Serious problem with drug trafficking; penalties for use and possession are severe.

Entry: You'll be issued with a one-month entry stamp in your passport on arrival. A six-month extension can be applied for.

Contact: www.dgo.gov.vg

Canada

Climate: This vast country has a continental climate, with hot summers and cold winters. Weather is more extreme with altitude, such as the Rocky Mountains, and proximity to the sea.

Safety: Low crime levels and excellent healthcare.

Entry: No visa needed.

Contact: www.london.gc.ca

Cayman Islands

Climate: Sub-tropical with warm temperatures year-round. Risk of hurricanes around September/October.

Safety: Low crime and excellent healthcare.

Entry: No visa needed.

Contact: Cayman Islands High Commission in London, 020 7491 7772.

Costa Rica

Climate: Hot and humid. Rainy season runs from May to November when severe flooding can occur.

Safety: Crime isn't much of a problem although it has increased slightly in recent years, mainly petty theft and pickpocketing against tourists. Malaria and dengue fever are prevalent. Very strong riptides pose a risk on the Atlantic coast and crocodiles on the Pacific coast, which is popular with surfers.

Entry: A valid UK passport allows stays of up to three months.

Contact: www.costarica.embassyhomepage.com

Cuba

Climate: Sub-tropical, warm year-round. Hurricane season runs from June to November.

Safety: Crime levels are low in this communist state, previously run by Fidel Castro. Petty theft occurs in Havana. Hepatitis and dengue fever are common, particularly in the summer months. Medical facilities are good but very expensive, and most be paid at the time, which can be up to £200 per day, so make sure you're covered.

Entry: Visa needed prior to arrival.

Contact: www.cubaldn.com

Dominica

Climate: Warm and humid year-round; tropical with high rainfall over the mountains.

Safety: Low crime rates and no major health risks. There is a danger from hurricanes, which can be devastating and are likely from June to November.

Entry: A valid UK passport allows up to six-month stays, although you must have a return air ticket.

Contact: www.dominica.embassyhomepage.com

Dominican Republic

Climate: Hot, humid and tropical along the coast; cooler in the highlands. Plenty of rain year-round.

Safety: Crime relatively low. Drug trafficking is a big problem and penalties for possession are severe including imprisonment in very harsh jail conditions. There has been a big increase in British nationals being arrested for trafficking, and the FCO warns all tourists to be vigilant about packing their own luggage and never carrying anything for anyone else. Risk of hurricanes between June and November.

Entry: No visa needed but you'll need a tourist card, available on arrival.

Contact: www.dominicanembassy.org.uk

Grenada

Climate: Hot and humid most of the year. Tradewinds help to relieve the humidity. Summer months from July to November are the wettest. Hurricane season from June to November.

Safety: Low crime, though avoid isolated beach areas after dark. Dengue fever occurs occasionally.

Entry: No visa needed for visits up to three months.

Contact: Grenada High Commission in London, 020 7385 4415.

Guadeloupe

Climate: Tropical, warm and humid year-round. Wettest months from May to November and hurricane season from June to November.

Safety: Crime levels low. Dengue fever common.

Entry: No visa needed.

Contact: Guadeloupe is a French overseas territory, www.ukinfrance.fco.gov.uk

Guatemala

Climate: On the Pacific and Caribbean coasts the climate is tropical; hot and humid. Dry season from October to May.

Safety: One of the highest crime rates in Latin America. Several armed attacks on tourists occurred in 2008 around major tourist sites like Tikai, Pete and Lake Atitlan, so be vigilant. There's also a risk of kidnapping at ATM machines and avoid travelling by public bus if possible as there have been cases of violent muggings.

Entry: No visa needed; UK passport allows 90-day visit.

Contact: Guatemala embassy, 020 7351 3042.

Hawaii

Climate: Tropical; warm year-round. Wetter in the mountains.

Safety: The islands are part of the USA and have a fairly low crime rate, although petty thefts do occur.

Entry: No visa needed.

Contact: www.usembassy.org.uk

Honduras

Climate: Tropical, hot and humid in coastal region; rain year-round particularly September to January.

Safety: High levels of crime; particular care should be taken travelling between towns and cities (bus jackings have occurred) and avoid walking alone on beaches and quieter areas at night. Malaria in remote, low-lying regions.

Entry: Brits can get a 30-day visit (tourist) visa on arrival, which can be extended by 30 days on two further occasions for a maximum of 90 days by applying to the immigration office.

Contact: www.ukinguatemala.gov.uk

Jamaica

Climate: Tropical, hot and humid around the coast; more temperate inland. Hurricane season runs from June to November. Warm year-round.

Safety: It has a high crime reputation, but much of the gang violence including shootings takes place in inner city neighbourhoods, such as West Kingston and parts of Montego Bay (not the resort area), away from tourist places. However, be alert for thieves and it's recommended not to use buses at night and only hire taxis approved by the Jamaica Tourist Board.

Entry: No visa needed.

Contact: www.jamaican.embassyhomepage.com

Martinique

Climate: Hot and humid for most of the year; rain most likely May to November. Wetter on the northeast side of the island. Hurricane season June to November.

Safety: Fairly low crime; petty theft, on beaches and from hotel rooms, does occur.

Entry: A department of France, no visa needed.

Contact: www.ambafrance-uk.org/

Mexico

Climate: Varied. The north and northwest are dry; far south and west, tropical. Central plateau, mild and temperate. Dry season October to March. Mountains on Caribbean side get rain year-round. Hurricane season runs from June to November.

Safety: Most visits are trouble-free, however street crime is on the increase and theft on buses is common. There have been incidences of kidnapping and reports of sexual attacks in Cancun and Mexico City. There were three shark attacks in 2008, all involving surfers.

Entry: No visa needed.

Contact: www.mexico.embassy-uk.co.uk

Montserrat

Climate: Tropical; hot and humid year-round. Wettest time is April and May. Hurricane season from June to November.

Safety: The biggest threat to tourist safety here is the Soufriere Hills Volcano which has been intermittently active since 1995. Low crime rate.

Entry: No visa needed.

Contact: Montserrat Government UK Office, 020 7031 0317.

Nicaragua

Climate: Pacific lowlands are hot and tropical; May to November rainy months. Cooler in the mountains.

Safety: Nicaragua has experienced a significant rise in thefts, break-ins and muggings. Street crime is prevalent in Managua. Don't travel on buses after dark and only use authorised taxis with red plates as there has been a rise in taxi muggings. Malaria is common.

Entry: No visa needed.

Contact: www.nicaragua.embassyhomepage.com

Panama

Climate: Dry season runs from January to April, rainy season May to December (the summer). Rainfall is lightest on Pacific coast.

Safety: Street crime risk, particularly in main shopping areas in Panama City. Occasional armed hold-ups. Avoid political demonstrations, which can flair up violently. Very severe penalties for even minor drug possession. Malaria and dengue fever are common in parts of the country.

Entry: No visa needed, but proof of onward journey.

Contact: www.panama.embassyhomepage.com

Puerto Rico

Climate: Hot summers, warm winters, rain falls throughout the year.

Safety: Low crime levels, but be aware of petty theft, like pickpocketing. Dengue fever occurs.

Entry: It's a self-governing commonwealth of the USA, so the same requirements; as of 12 January 2009, you need to register at least three days in advance if you plan to visit, plus you will be required to be photographed and fingerprinted on arrival.

Contact: www.usembassy.org.uk

St Lucia

Climate: Tropical; hot and humid. The hurricane season in St Lucia normally runs from June to November.

Safety: Violent crime is a problem within local communities. Crimes against tourists aren't frequent but include muggings and thefts from hotels or yachts. Dengue fever is endemic to Latin America and the Caribbean and can occur throughout the year.

Entry: No visa needed; valid UK passport allows stays up to 42 days.

Contact: www.stlucia.embassyhomepage.com

St Vincent & The Grenadines

Climate: See St Lucian.
Safety: See St Lucia.
Entry: No visa needed.
Contact: St Vincent & The Grenadines High Commission, 020 7565 2874.

Trinidad & Tobago

Climate: Tropical; hot and humid year-round with no major extremes. Rains throughout the year, particularly June to November.
Safety: Trinidad: High level of gang related violence and crime. However, incidents are concentrated in the inner city neighbourhoods east of Port of Spain's city centre, particularly Laventille, Morvant and Barataria. Increase in violent crime, muggings, robberies and kidnapping for ransom in all areas in 2008. There have also been attacks, some involving firearms, at tourist sites, including Fort George, the Pitch Lake, although these are rare. Tobago: Much lower crime level, robberies do occur.
Entry: No visa needed.
Contact: www.trinidad.embassyhomepage.com

Turks & Caicos Islands

Climate: Warm throughout the year; no rainy season. Hurricane season runs from August to November.
Safety: Low crime rate. Hurricane risk, it has been hit severely in the past.
Entry: No visa needed.
Contact: The T&C is a UK dependent territory, see www.fco.gov.uk

United States of America

Climate: Varied. Mostly temperate, but tropical in Hawaii and Florida, arctic in Alaska, semi-arid in the great plains west of the Mississippi River, and arid in the Great Basin of the southwest; low winter temperatures in the northwest are occasionally affected in January and February by warm Chinook winds from the eastern slopes of the Rocky Mountains.

Safety: General terrorism threat. Crime levels vary from state to state.

Entry: The US has announced new measures that require all those travelling under the Visa Waiver Programme to provide details online 72 hours prior to travel; known as an Electronic Travel System or ESTA. This became compulsory on 12 January 2009. For more information, and to apply online go to https://esta.cbp.dhs.gov.

Contact: www.usembassy.org.uk/

US Virgin Islands

Climate: Tropical; hot and humid for most of the year. Wetter on the northeast side of the islands, May to September has the heaviest rainfall.

Safety: Low crime levels, occasional petty theft.

Entry: No visa required (see above).

Contact: www.usembassy.org.uk/

SOUTH AMERICA

Argentina

Climate: A vast country, with a climate that ranges from humid tropical forests in the north to dry and arid plains in Patagonia and snow and glaciers in the Andes and far south.

Safety: Relatively safe, though high crime rates in major cities and urban areas.

Entry: No visa required.

Contact: www.argentine-embassy.uk.org

Bolivia

Climate: Hot and humid in the north and west. Wettest in the summer months, from November to February; winter months from April to October are drier and temperatures pleasant. La Paz gets daily rain.

Safety: Unstable political situation with regular demonstrations, riots and roadblocks. It's also the third largest producer of cocaine in the world, so drug trafficking is a major problem. High crime rates, from muggings to kidnappings, particularly foreign visitors. High incidence of malaria in the lowland tropical areas.

Entry: No visa needed, but length of stay limited to 30 days although 60-day extensions can be requested.

Contact: www.boembassy-london.com

Brazil

Climate: A vast country (the fifth largest in the world) with several climate zones. The Amazon Basin is hot and humid year-round; rainy season from April to July. The south has hot summers and cool winters. The Andean mountains can be severely cold.

Safety: High crime and violence levels, particularly in the major cities such as Rio. Keep out of the *favelas* (slums), which tend to be lawless, unless you are with a guide. Drugs and drug gangs are a major problem. Brazil also has a problem with tropical diseases; malaria, dengue fever and yellow fever are widespread.

Entry: No visa needed. Maximum stay 90 days, but you must show sufficient evidence of money to support your visit, details of accommodation and return travel documents.

Contact: www.brazil.org.uk

Chile

Climate: Mainly temperate, although very arid in the north in the Atacama desert – the driest in the world.

Safety: Low crime levels, but pickpocketing is a common problem in the main cities and tourist sites.

Entry: Valid UK passport will allow you entry for 90 days.

Contact: www.chile.embassyhomepage.com

Colombia

Climate: Warm and tropical in the lowlands on the Caribbean and Pacific coasts; cooler in the highlands. Most rain falls from March to May and October/November.

Safety: The FCO advises against travel in some areas of the country which are controlled by armed gangs. Crime is high and violent; kidnapping of foreigners is a problem with backpackers being at risk. Drug trafficking is a major problem as Colombia is the world's largest (illegal) producer of cocaine. Yellow fever, dengue fever and malaria are common.

Entry: You can enter the country for up to 60 days with a valid UK passport, no visa needed; extensions are possible. Valid yellow fever certificate and valid return travel ticket required.

Contact: www.colombianembassy.co.uk

Ecuador

Climate: Hot, humid and tropical on the coast, cooler in the mountains. Wettest months, January to May.

Safety: The FCO advises against all travel in the Colombia border areas. High crime in some areas, including kidnapping. Trekkers and backpackers should be wary. Malaria and dengue fever are a risk in the coastal and jungle areas. Capital city Quito is one of the highest in the world so there is a risk of altitude sickness and in the Andes; acclimatise slowly.

Entry: Laws have just changed and a visa is no longer required for British nationals. UK passport allows you to stay for up to 90 days.

Contact: Ecuador Embassy, 020 7584 2648

Falkland Islands

Climate: Temperate and windy. The winter months (December and January) can be very wet and cold.

Safety: Crime virtually non-existent and no major health risks.

Entry: No visa needed, but return air ticket and pre-booked accommodation are required for entry.

Contact: www.falklands.gov.fk/

French Guiana

Climate: Tropical, hot, wet and humid in the lowlands. Cooler in the highlands. Rainy season from December to June.

Safety: Rural French Guiana is relatively safe; the larger towns aren't particularly safe to wander around at night. Increase in crime and drug trafficking in recent years, police roadblocks and searches are common.

Entry: It's a department of France, so is a member of the EU and no visa is needed. You will need a yellow fever vaccination certificate.

Contact: www.ambafrance-uk.org

Guyana

Climate: Hot, wet and humid in the lowlands; cooler in the highlands. Two rainy seasons, April to August and November to January.

Safety: Fairly high crime levels, including shootings, armed robberies and carjackings. Exercise caution in Georgetown and avoid any outward signs of wealth. Malaria risk.

Entry: No visa needed, but you must have an onward or return air ticket. Yellow fever vaccination required if you're arriving from an infected country.

Paraguay

Climate: Sub-tropical; hot and rain fairly constant throughout the year. Humid summers, December to March; mild winters.

Safety: Relatively safe, although violent crime is on the increase particularly in cities at night. Malaria, rabies, diphtheria and yellow fever occur.

Entry: No visa needed but proof of onward journey required.

Contact: www.paraguayembassy.co.uk

Peru

Climate: Varied. Coastal plains have a desert climate and are very hot and dry from January to March. The Andes has a dry season from May to September when days are warm but nights cold; what little rain there is in the mountains falls mainly from December to May. In the eastern lowlands, the climate is hot and humid year-round.

Safety: Relatively safe, although theft is prevalent in cities and on public transport. Malaria, rabies and yellow fever occur.

Entry: No visa required.

Contact: www.peruembassy-uk.com

Suriname

Climate: Tropical; hot and humid with lots of rain, particularly from April to July.

Safety: Armed robbery and violent crime are frequent in Paramaribo. Pickpocketing and mugging occurs in shopping districts; walking alone at night isn't recommended in the capital. Dengue fever risk, malaria common.

Entry: Visa needed in advance of travel. If you are arriving from Guyana, French Guiana or Brazil you are required to show proof of a yellow fever vaccination.

Contact: There's no UK embassy but information can be obtained from the Suriname Consulate in Amsterdam; 0011 31 206 426 137.

Uruguay

Climate: Warm summers, mild winters. Moderate rainfall year-round.

Safety: Generally trouble free, with a low risk of terrorism and no political instability. There are occurrences of street crime in Montevideo, but police patrols are active and act as a good deterrent. Dengue fever risk.

Entry: No visa needed.

Contact: www.uruguay.embassyhomepage.com

Venezuela

Climate: Tropical; hot and humid, cooler in the highlands. Wettest (and hottest) time from May to August.

Safety: The FCO advises against all travel to within 80km (50 miles) of the Colombian border in the states of Zulia, Tachira and Apure. Terrorist and illegal armed groups are active in these states and there is a risk of kidnapping. High incidence of street crime. Road to and from the airport to Caracas is dangerous and there have been incidences of muggings and kidnappings by bogus taxi drivers from the airport.

Entry: No visa needed for stays up to 90 days.

Contact: www.venezuela.embassyhomepage.com

DANGER ZONE

These countries are ones that the Foreign & Commonwealth Office has advised (at the time of writing) that British nationals shouldn't visit unless it's absolutely essential due to the high safety risks.

Afghanistan

Climate: Extreme; hot, dry summers and severe winters – minus temperatures and lots of snow.

Safety: The FCO advises against all travel; high threat of terrorism.

Entry: British nationals must obtain a visa before entering the country.

Contact: www.afghanistanembassyuk.org/

Algeria

Climate: Very hot most of the year, although the coast enjoys a Mediterranean climate. Over four-fifths of the country is covered by the Sahara Desert.

Safety: The FCO advises against all but essential travel. Terrorism remains a high threat.

Entry: You must obtain a visa from the Algerian embassy in London before travelling.

Contact: www.algerianembassy.org.uk

Angola

Climate: Very hot and humid; travel in the rainy season is difficult.

Safety: Serious crime and violence is a major problem everywhere, including kidnapping of foreigners. The FCO advises against all but essential travel.

Entry: New visa regulations have come into force and a visa must now be obtained before entering the country. If you overstay there are heavy fines.

Contact: Angola Embassy, 020 7299 9850.

Armenia

Climate: Warm summers, very cold winters. Rain falls year-round.

Safety: The FCO is currently advising against all but essential travel, particularly near the border with Azerbaijan where there is a tense military situation. Sporadic fighting and violent political situation sometimes leading to street demonstrations and rioting. Foreigners are prone to be victims of pickpocketing and mugging in the cities.

Entry: Visa required, which can be obtained on arrival at main airports and land border crossings.

Contact: www.armenia.embassyhomepage.com

Azerbaijan

Climate: The natural climatic conditions of Azerbaijan are unique, with nine out of 11 climatic zones. Dry, subtropical with hot summers and mild winters; alpine tundra in the mountains

Safety: The FCO is advising against all but essential travel here, particularly to military occupied areas. Surprisingly, crime levels are fairly low, but corruption is an everyday aspect of life. There have been outbreaks of rabies and malaria in the south.

Entry: Visa needed. Single visa entry (up to 30 days) can be obtained at Baku Airport for £63. There are fines for illegal overstays. You can't enter or leave the country via the land borders with Russia.

Contact: www.azembassy.org.uk

Burundi

Climate: Temperate climate, with two rainy seasons.

Safety: Politically unstable and very violent. There's no British Embassy. Malaria and cholera are prevalent and healthcare is non-existent. The FCO strongly recommends against travel here.

Entry: Visa needed and obtainable on arrival. You have to register your presence with the Belgian Embassy in Bujumbura.

Contact: www.britishembassykigali.org.rw

Central African Republic

Climate: Hot and dry in the north (Sahara desert). The south has fairly heavy rain year-round, particularly June to October and high humidity.

Safety: Politically unstable; outside the capital Bangui the country is lawless and violent.

Entry: Visa required; yellow fever vaccination certificate required.

Contact: There is no UK embassy in the CAR and no CAR representation in the UK.

Chad

Climate: Most of the country is arid and mountainous and it's hot year-round.

Safety: The political situation is very unstable and violent. Crime levels high, healthcare minimal and there are lots of tropical diseases.

Entry: Visa needed and yellow fever vaccination certificate.

Contact: No UK embassy in Chad and no Chad representation in the UK. Contact via the Chadian embassy in Brussels.

Congo

Climate: Equatorial climate; high temperatures and heavy rainfall.

Safety: Formerly the Belgian Congo, the country has had a very violent past since independence in 1960. Very unstable politically with vicious civil wars. At present there's a large UN peacekeeping force maintaining an uneasy truce, but the situation changes all the time and the FCO advises against all but essential travel there. Crime levels are very high and violent, with foreigners at real risk. Malaria, cholera, ebola and typhoid are common. Medical facilities are non-existent outside city of Kinshasa.

Entry: Visa needed before travel and yellow fever vaccination certificate.

Contact: Embassy of Democratic Republic of the Congo, 020 7960 6277.

Haiti

Climate: Tropical; hot and humid, rain year-round.

Safety: The FCO advises against all but essential travel. High crime including random civilian shootings, violence and kidnappings of foreigners for ransom. Unstable political situation with sporadic violent demonstrations and riots over the high price of food. Hurricane season from June to November, Haiti was hit very hard in 2008 resulting in mudslides and flooding, causing many deaths. Malaria, dengue fever and hepatitis are common.

Entry: No visa required.

Contact: There's no Haitian Embassy in the UK, but there is one in Paris which visitors are advised to contact before travelling, 0033 01 4763 4778.

Iran

Climate: Arid, desert climate, with very hot summers and cold winters (December to April). Temperatures range from –20 to 50 degrees.

Safety: High terrorism threat and the FCO advises against all travel within 100km (60 miles) of the Iran/Afghanistan border and within 10km (6 miles) of the Iran/Iraq border. The Pakistan border is also insecure. Political demonstrations sometimes turn violent. There have been previous incidents of foreigners being arrested and detained by Iranian authorities. Street crime in Tehran is low, although robberies do occur. There have been incidents of kidnapping of foreigners by armed gangs in southeastern Iran.

Entry: Visa needed and should be lodged well in advance from www.iran-embassy.org.uk

Contact: It's strongly advised that you register with the British Embassy in Tehran, www.britishembassy.gov.uk/iran

Iraq

Climate: Very hot, dry summers and mild winters. Low rainfall all year.

Safety: Most of the country is a no-go area for British tourists, with a high threat of terrorism and kidnap everywhere. If you must go, it's advised that you arrange your own professional security.

Entry: Visa needed.

Contact: www.iraqmofa.net

Liberia

Climate: Very hot year-round; rainy season runs from May to October and June to July.

Safety: Travel to all areas outside capital Monrovia is discouraged due to the high level of protests over political developments, salaries and working conditions which can flair up at any time; UN peacekeeping forces patrol the cities and roads. Violent crime, which the police have limited capability to prevent, is rife in Monrovia, which you should not walk around alone at night. It's advised to arrange private security if you must travel here. Malaria and waterborne diseases are common.

Entry: Visa needed before travel.

Contact: www.embassyofliberia.org.uk

Mauritania

Climate: Hot and dry. Rain falls year-round but particularly December to April, when cyclones can occur.

Safety: Following a military coup in August 2008, the FCO advises against all but essential travel to Mauritania. There is a high threat of kidnapping in

Mauritania by Al Qa'ida in the Islamic Maghreb (AQIM), particularly outside the main urban areas.

Entry: Visa needed prior to travel.

Contact: www.mauritania.embassyhomepage.com

Somalia

Climate: Hot and humid in the north coast, elsewhere very dry.

Safety: The FCO advises against all travel here due to the level of ongoing serious violence, including murder, kidnapping and armed robbery, and internal insecurity. High threat of terrorism.

Entry: Visa needed.

Contact: There's no British representation in Somalia, and the Somalia Embassy is closed in the UK due to the civil war. Contact the British Embassy in Addis Ababa: britishembassy.addisababa@fco.gov.

Yemen

Climate: Hot, desert conditions. Southern coast gets very little rain and is hot and humid year-round. Central highlands are mild and dry, any rain falls in March and April and August. Winter nights can be very cold.

Safety: High threat of terrorism. The FCO advises against all but essential travel to the Governorates of Sa'dah, Ma'rib, al Jawf, Shabwah and Hadramaut due to the threat of terrorism and tribal violence. There have been a number of kidnappings of foreigners in the past. It's strongly recommended that travel outside the major cities is only undertaken with an organised group accompanied by a military escort.

Entry: Visa needed.

Contact: www.yemenembassy.org.uk

Zimbabwe

Climate: Tropical; pleasant and warm year-round. Wet season from November to March/April when it's very humid.

Safety: Due to the continuing unstable political situation, the FCO advises against all travel to high density, low-income suburban areas at any time; and all but essential travel to Harare city centre, rural Manicaland and farming areas. Reports of gangs of army personnel beating people, confiscating money and carrying out random arrests in the centre of Harare. Mugging, pickpocketing and jewellery theft are common in Harare and other city centres, especially after dark. Armed carjackings are on the increase as the economy gets worse.

Entry: Visa needed.

Contact: www.zimbabwe.embassyhomepage.com

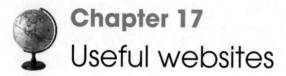

Chapter 17
Useful websites

Accommodation

www.couchsurfing.com

www.expedia.co.uk

www.travelsupermarket.com

www.podhotel.com

www.yotel.com

www.cube-hotels.com

www.i-escape.com

www.hiphotels.com

www.sawdays.co.uk

www.ecohotelsoftheworld.com

www.hostelworld.com

www.hihostels.com

www.yha.org.uk

www.Helpx.net

www.homebase-hols.com

www.homeexchange.com

www.campingo.com

www.tunehotels.com

www.capsuleinn.com

www.travelintelligence.com

www.mrandmrssmith.com
www.tablethotels.com
www.epoquehotels.com
www.hipmarrakech.com

Boat trips
www.malawi-travel.com
www.emeraldstar.ie
www.steppestravel.co.uk
www.strandtravel.co.uk
www.freightertrips.com

Cycling
www.ctc.org.uk

Fear of flying
www.flyingwithoutfear.info

Flashpacking
www.flashpackerguide.info

Flights
www.opodo.com
www.foundem.com
www.statravel.co.uk

Foreign & Commonwealth Office
www.fco.gov.uk/travel

Gap years
www.globalxperience.com

www.gapyear.com
www.realgap.co.uk
www.gapwork.com
www.statravel.co.uk
www.gogapyear.com

Green travel
www.co2balance.uk.com
www.carbonneutral.com
www.climatecare.org
www.carbonfootprint.com
www.intrepidtravel.com
www.ecotravelling.co.uk
www.responsibletravel.com
www.ecohotelsoftheworld.com
www.greentraveller.co.uk

Health
www.jungleformula.co.uk
www.netdoctor.co.uk
www.who.int
www.travelhealth.co.uk

Insurance
www.direct-travel.co.uk
www.atlasdirect.co.uk
www.gotravelinsurance.co.uk
www.ehic.org.uk

Keeping in touch
www.gmail.com

www.mail.yahoo.com
www.hotmail.com
eu.blackberry.com/eng/
www.skype.com
www.facebook.com
www.cybercafes.com

Language classes
www.bbc.co.uk/languages

Learning
www.creative-escapes.co.uk
www.whydontyou.com
www.statravel.co.uk
www.danceholidays.com

Passport
www.ips.gov.uk

Planning
www.tripit.com
www.google.co.uk
www.kayak.co.uk
www.thebigtravelguide.com
www.postoffice.co.uk

Rail
www.interrail.net
www.railaustralia.com.au
www.indianrail.gov.in
www.thailandbytrain.com

www.japanrailpass.net
www.seat61.com
www.trans-siberia.com
www.amtrak.com
www.eurostar.com

Road trips
www.savannahway.com.au
www.hertz.co.uk
www.avis.co.uk
www.theaa.com
www.rac.co.uk

Sabbaticals
www.gapyyearforgrownups.co.uk/sabbatical

Short breaks
www.contiki.co.uk
www.indialine.com
www.statravel.co.uk/

Solo travel
www.travellingalone.co.uk
www.thelmaandlouise.com
www.explore.co.uk
www.intrepidtravel.com
www.letstrekaustralia.com
www.trekamerica.com

Spiritual/wellbeing
www.amritapuri.org/ashram

www.buddhanet.info
www.bodyandsoulholidays.info
www.nealsyardagency.com
www.wellbeingescapes.co.uk
www.lotusjourneys.com
www.lifecraft.co.uk
www.inspa-retreats.com
www.hoho.co.uk/detox.html
www.yogatraveller.com
www.yogatravel.co.uk
www.responsibletravel.com

Travel guides
www.worldtravelguide.net
www.wordtravels.com
www.tripadvisor.co.uk
www.guardian.co.uk/travel
www.cntraveller.co.uk

Volunteering
www.VSO.org.uk
www.statravel.i-to-i.com
www.earthwatch.org
www.biosphere-expeditions.org
www.bunac.org.uk
www.do-it.org.uk

Weather
www.weatherbase.com
www.worldclimate.com

Working abroad

www.nannyjob.co.uk
www.gapyear.com/carework
www.thompson.co.uk/jobs/
www.pickingjobs.com
www.kibbutz.org.il/eng/
www.natives.co.uk
www.bunac.org/uk/kampusa
www.bunac.org.uk
www.tefltraining.co.uk
www.tefl.co.uk
www.cactustefl.com
www.onlinetefl.com
www.oxfordtefl.com
www.jetprogramme.org

Index